I0108883

UNLOCKING
THE POWER
OF YOU

JOHN W. STANKO

Unlocking the Power of You
by John W. Stanko

Copyright ©2016, 2022 John W. Stanko

All rights reserved. This book is protected under the copyright laws of the United States of America. This book may not be copied or reprinted for commercial gain or profit.

Unless otherwise identified, Scripture quotations are taken from THE HOLY BIBLE: New International Version ©1978 by the New York International Bible Society, used by permission of Zondervan Bible Publishers.

Scriptures marked AMP are taken from The Amplified Bible, Old Testament. Copyright 1965, 1987, by The Zondervan Corporation.

Scriptures marked MSG are taken from THE MESSAGE. Copyright © by Eugene H. Peterson 1993, 1994, 1995, 1996, 2000, 2002. Used by permission of NavPress Publishing Group.

Scriptures marked NAS are taken from the New American Standard Bible, Copyright ©1960, 1962, 1963, 1968, 1971, 1973, 1975, 1977 by The Lockman Foundation.

Scripture marked NKJ are taken from the New King James Version. Copyright © 1982 by Thomas Nelson, Inc. Scripture marked NLT are taken from the Holy Bible, New Living Translation, copyright ©1996. Used by permission of Tyndale House Publishers, Inc., Wheaton IL 60189.

Scripture marked TLB are taken from The Living Bible by Kenneth N. Taylor, Used by permission of Tyndale House, Wheaton, IL. All are used by permission. All rights reserved.

ISBN 978-1-63360-032-4

For Worldwide Distribution
Printed in the U.S.A.

Urban Press
P.O. Box 8881
Pittsburgh, PA 15221-0881
412.646.2780

Table of Contents

Introduction

You are holding in your hand the fourth and final installment in my Unlocking book series. The first three were:

- *Unlocking the Power of Your Purpose*
- *Unlocking the Power of Your Creativity*
- *Unlocking the Power of Your Productivity*

This book, *Unlocking the Power of You*, is birthed out of my work over the years with many people who have sought help to find their purpose. I would sit with them and listen, often administering a battery of personality assessments, then providing feedback to help them connect the dots that would show them their purpose. I have done that with thousands of people, and I noticed one interesting theme that ran through many of my coaching sessions. I found that most people are fighting against themselves and their purpose!

What do I mean by this? As we would talk, I would hear people make comments like: "I need to be more organized," "I am not very outgoing," or "I can't finish what I start." When people made those statements, they were convinced that they had to undergo massive personality reconstruction before God could ever use them. This conclusion was based in the fear that their deficiencies disabled them from doing much without extensive improvement.

My experience, however, has shown me that God is much more comfortable with your humanity than you are. He is ready to use you now. That doesn't mean you don't require extensive personal development; it simply means that God can and wants to use you while you are under reconstruction. This truth was reinforced in my mind when I was in a southern city working with Miguel (not his real name).

Miguel approached me for help, explaining that he had been hired and fired from 14 jobs in the previous three years! What's more, Miguel was pretty sure he was about to lose number 15 in the days to come! Miguel begged for a session, explaining that he was married with three children and needed to get and keep a job. I was not hopeful that I could help, and I warned him that I was not a career counselor, just a purpose coach.

In the days leading up to our meeting, I mentioned to the pastor of the church where I was working that I was getting together with Miguel. The pastor lost all expression in his face as he warned me, "Don't have anything to do with that guy." I said that I knew Miguel had problems holding a job, and the pastor responded, "Yes, and one of those jobs he recently lost was a position he had here at the church. We had to let him go! He is unemployable!"

Then I ran into Miguel's wife who gave me the same report I had heard from Miguel. "Pastor," she said plaintively, "my husband has lost 14 jobs in the last three years and I think he is about to lose number 15. Help us!" Armed with that confirming information, I entered my meeting with Miguel trusting God for a breakthrough.

After we did the personality assessments, I immediately saw the problem. Miguel was one of the most spontaneous, creative, and disorganized. What's more, he had these characteristics to the extreme and had been diagnosed with adult Attention Deficit Disorder (ADD). He never met a detail that he enjoyed, so he simply ignored them. For example, it was not a matter of what time Miguel would arrive for work, it was a matter of what day he would show up. He was always late, and thus had been labeled as irresponsible and flakey.

We did the personality assessments and I was able to describe Miguel's personality to him before he was able to tell me. I told him that it is almost impossible for him to finish anything because he would become so bored so quickly that he would lose interest almost immediately once the excitement and novelty wore off.

Then I said this: "There are only a few things you have to finish in life. One, is your walk with the Lord. The other is your marriage commitment to your wife. The third is your care for your children, although that will diminish as they get older." Then I asked, "So who said you have to get and keep a job for five years? Why is that the standard?"

Miguel looked at me with astonishment and said, "Then what kind of job should I look for?"

I know my answer disappointed him when I replied, "I don't know, Miguel. Let's pray that God will help you find something that is perfectly suited for you. Maybe you should start your own company." We prayed and I didn't see him until four months later when he picked me up at the airport.

When I got into his car, Miguel was super excited. He had started a consulting business, had one big client and was making money. He gave me three business cards with his name on it, each representing a role he played in the company. "I'm bringing home money already and my wife is happy," Miguel gushed. "Now, I want to help you with your company!"

I smiled but politely deflected his offer of help. After all, this was a man who had recently lost 15 jobs, and I didn't really think he had anything to offer me. When I returned to his city four months after that, Miguel had started another company (and had three more business cards). He moved his family into a beautiful new home where he took me after he picked me up. His wife ran out to greet me and said, "I don't know what you did, but we are so grateful, and Miguel wants to help you! We both want to help you!"

I expressed delight in their newfound success, but I was still not enthusiastic about Miguel's input. Finally, I brought him along to witness one of my seminar sessions and then we went back to his office—yes, he had rented a full suite of offices for his team—to debrief what he had seen. His short evaluation was, "Your stuff is brilliant, but you don't know what you are doing!"

One half of me wanted to smack Miguel upside his head! How dare he talk to me like that? I was twice his age and had so much more life experience, and had helped him get to where he was. The other half of me had to agree with him. I didn't know how to package, market or present my seminar material. After a long discussion, I retained Miguel's services and he helped me strategize a business model that helped me maximize my impact and revenue. Who would have thought it possible? I certainly did not (just another example of what Miguel said: I didn't know what I was doing).

I will spare you the details of Miguel's next five years that included leaving the companies he had started to move to another country with his family. He returned home to the U.S. after 18 months and moved to New England, then to Florida, and finally back to the city where I had first met him. After his return, we would meet in a restaurant where he conducted all his new business. Later, he bought a controlling interest in the restaurant, which he sold one year later. Today he has another business that is perfectly suited to his upbeat, high-energy, easily-bored style.

What helped Miguel become so successful? He stopped fighting who he was and not only stopped fighting it, he embraced it. He stopped waiting for changes to who he was that would never happen. It's true that he had a unique personality with extreme characteristics, but he stopped trying to fix those and looked for ways to make them work on his behalf. Miguel came to grips with the possibility that his personality was exactly who God wanted him to be, as unusual as that style was. As long as he fulfilled his family responsibilities, he was free to express his personality in any way that was ethical and successful.

I have discovered this same tendency in many others, although not to the extent as Miguel. I have met people who believe they must be more patient for God to use them.

Yet, God often wants to use their impatience to help combat homelessness, hunger or child trafficking, issues that should not be tolerated but "impatiently" pursued and eradicated. I have talked with some who want to achieve something great, but feel their ambition is ungodly. It is exactly their visionary style, however, that God uses to establish something significant that will touch many lives.

I could go on, but you get the idea. This book is designed to help you combat your own tendency to work against who you are and to wait for God to change you into a person He never intended you to be. Throughout this book, I will share my own stories of how I became comfortable with who I am and who I am not. We will look at many biblical examples of those who went through the same process.

You can read this book straight through at your own pace, or focus on one chapter every week for the next 52 weeks, just like the other three Unlocking books. I have not grouped the entries into sections with themes, although a few of them do flow sequentially as a two- to five-part series. Therefore, you can jump around from chapter to chapter or start with the first chapter and finish with fifty-two.

God made you the way you are. You must free yourself not from your personality traits and quirks but from the effects that selfishness has had on those traits. If you look to stay up late and that's how you work best, stop fighting yourself! If you need a lot of alone time to recharge your batteries, then go off alone as often as you need. If you love to watch movies, then do it and seek God for how He wants to use and direct that interest.

If you like the color orange, as I do, then feel free to own as many orange-colored items as makes you happy. There are times when it would be wrong to insist that it always be your way, but that isn't wrong all the time. It's up to you to find, with God's help, when to pick up your cross and deny yourself and when it's time to stay true to who God made you to be.

You will unlock tremendous power when you stop

trying to change things that God is not interested in changing. God has an assignment for you that is perfectly suited to who He made you to be. This book will help you find your personality sweet spot and accept that assignment. The world is waiting for you to unlock and release the power inherent in your personality. I am confident this book will help you do just that.

John W. Stanko
Pittsburgh, Pennsylvania USA
February 2016

The Five Regrets of the Dying

A few years ago I ran across an article written by an Australian writer, Bronnie Ware, who had devoted many hours to working with patients who are dying. Here is a summary of her journey that led up to her writing the essay:

> After too many years of unfulfilling work, Bronnie Ware began searching for a job with heart. Despite having no formal qualifications or experience, she found herself working in palliative care. Over the years she spent tending to the needs of those who were dying, Bronnie's life was transformed. Later, she wrote an Internet blog about the most common regrets expressed to her by the people she had cared for. The article, also called "The Top Five Regrets of the Dying", gained so much momentum that it was read by more than three million people around the globe in its first year.

In this chapter, I want to summarize the five points from Bronnie's article, and then focus on one point in particular.

THE FIVE REGRETS

Here are the five regrets that Bronnie discovered in working with those patients close to death over the years:

1. I wish I'd had the courage to live a life true to myself, not the life others expected of me.

2. I wish I didn't work so hard.

3. I wish I'd had the courage to express my feelings.

4. I wish I had stayed in touch with my friends.

5. I wish that I had let myself be happier.

Here is what Ware had to say about the first point, the courage to be true to self and not others:

> This was the most common regret of all. When people realize that their life is almost over and look back clearly on it, it is easy to see how many dreams have gone unfulfilled. Most people have had not honored even a half of their dreams and had to die knowing that it was due to choices they had made, or not made. It is very important to try and honor at least some of your dreams along the way. From the moment that you lose your health, it is too late. Health brings a freedom very few realize, until they no longer have it.

DON'T LET IT BE YOUR REGRET

It takes courage to be true to yourself and who God created you to be. When David went out to fight Goliath, King Saul tried to have David wear his (Saul's) battle armor. Saul was a tall man, however, and the armor didn't fit. David did not try to please the king. Instead he rejected the armor and took along his sling shot, something that was more true to who he was. His success of course is legendary (see 1 Samuel 17:38-40).

Are you wearing someone else's armor? If you are, then you are headed for the number one regret expressed by the dying according to Bronnie Ware's research. I cannot say what you should do, but I can urge you to follow your heart and stop living your life for someone else, unless it is for the Lord. I was challenged by this list and I hope you are, too. Now that you have read it, it's time to get about the work of living before it's too late.

What to Do with Your Big Head

How do you react when you do something well? What's more, how do you handle it when someone compliments you for something they admire about you? If you're like some, you may not know what to do in those situations. You don't want to appear proud or egocentric, so you may actually try to minimize your strengths and achievements in your eyes and in the eyes of others. This may seem spiritual or noble, but it's actually detrimental to your ongoing development and growth.

What should you do when you succeed or receive a compliment? I'm glad you asked. For the answer, however, you have to read on.

A BIG HEAD

When David got ready to face Goliath, he made specific and graphic declarations of what he was about to do to Goliath (see 1 Samuel 17). David made good on his promises, killing Goliath with one stone from his slingshot. It's what he did next that answers the questions I raised above.

David cut off Goliath's head! That was one big head not only to cut off but also to carry around. The armies of Israel were encouraged by David's victory, and went forth to win a great victory over the Philistine army. That was one by-product of David's success. Then David did something else that would be quite uncharacteristic for most of us: "David took the Philistine's head and brought it to Jerusalem, and he put the Philistine's weapons in his own tent" (1 Samuel 17:54).

What did David do with the head? I doubt if he kept it in his tent or made a keychain out of it. He did what most champions did with such spoils of battle. David probably impaled Goliath's head on a post for everyone to see. David celebrated his victory and advertised his achievement! What's more, he kept a souvenir of the battle by keeping the giant's sword in his trophy case.

How does that answer the question of what to do when you achieve success? How does this give you insight into how you should respond when you receive a compliment?

DON'T WORRY THAT A BIG HEAD WILL GIVE YOU A BIG HEAD

David wanted people to see Goliath's head so they would be encouraged to fight their own battles. As any good leader, David wanted the people to see that they didn't have to cower in fear. More importantly, David didn't minimize his success. He didn't say, "Well, it was nothing. You know, it was a lucky shot and God really did it, it wasn't me. You could have done the same thing." Instead, David said, "Look what I've done. What can you do? If this is what God helped me do, what will He help you do?" That's what you need to do as well. If someone compliments you for something you've done or something you are, respond by saying, "Thank you, and I thank God for His help." Don't push their praise away, but allow them to admire you and learn from your example.

If you have done something and no one compliments you, then compliment yourself! Admire what you've done. Savor the moment, without being self-conscious or worrying about what others would think of you, or that God is displeased. If you achieve a goal for which you have worked hard, throw yourself a party and invite your friends to celebrate with you. Go out to dinner or take a trip in honor God for your promotion, earned degree or completed project.

David knew how to celebrate his victories and use them to spur himself and others on to greater things. You and I need to do the same. Don't worry about a big head; there will be enough tough knocks and challenges to keep your feet firmly planted in reality.

Thinking like this will help you see that you are not really afraid of failure, but afraid of success—of what you will do if and when you succeed! Can you handle success and the admiration of others? I hope you will learn to broadcast your victories rather than hide behind mediocrity so that no one is offended and you aren't uncomfortable. Aim for great things, do them and tell the world when you succeed.

Your Strengths and Weaknesses

I am a proponent of functioning in your strengths rather than trying to build up your weaknesses. It makes sense to me that God gives you gifts and talents, which are your strength, and He want you to exercise them as often as possible for the good of others. If you don't have the strength of singing, for example, you don't want to go solo in front of your congregation. This is an easy-to-comprehend example, yet I still find people reluctant to talk about or develop their strengths, especially in light of what Paul wrote about functioning in weakness:

> Three times I pleaded with the Lord to take it away from me. But he said to me, "My grace is sufficient for you, for my power is made perfect in *weakness*." Therefore, I will boast all the more gladly about my *weaknesses*, so that Christ's power may rest on me. That is why, for Christ's sake, I delight in *weaknesses*, in insults, in hardships, in persecutions, in difficulties. For when I am *weak*, then I am strong (2 Corinthians 12:8-10, emphasis added).

How can we resolve these words about weakness with my admonition to function in your strengths? Until I hosted a recent purpose seminar, I did not know how to resolve it.

During the seminar, we determined that purpose is the answer to your important "*what*" question—*what* should I do with my life? Those in attendance saw that we often derail our consideration of the *what* by thinking about the *how* question—*how* can I possibly support myself and my family by doing this? *how* will it all work out? *how* can I possibly do this at my age (young or old)?

I wrote *what* and *how* on a white board when one of the young ladies in the seminar offered this perspective: "It seems that the *what* is your strength, but the *how* is your weakness. We must accept the *what* but then trust the Lord for the *how*." And I thought, "That's it!"

Look back at what Paul wrote in 2 Corinthians. His weakness was the *how* of his purpose to the Gentiles. He encountered persecution, difficulties and the insults from many – he was clear on the *what* he was given to do, but the *how* was his challenge. He faced opposition on every front and even had to face his own physical limitations that limited his energy. It was in his *how* weakness that the Lord was exalted as He empowered Paul to fulfill his purpose.

Paul saw that he was in his best position for success when he functioned in his purpose, while also facing his limitations and trusting the Lord to somehow make a way. God always did make a way, even when he was in prison or on a sinking ship. When the ship to Rome was going down, Paul was fulfilling his purpose of taking the gospel to the Gentiles as he preached and witnessed to the ship's Gentile crew.

This understanding is important for your PurposeQuest. If you are going to face life's difficulties, you need your purpose strength. At the same time, you will face your own inadequacies and the problems of life that will make your purpose seem like a dream. You will ask the Lord for help with the how, for that is your point of weakness. When He sends help, you will say, like Paul, that you glory in your weaknesses while you function in your strengths.

The Parable of the Pencil

A radio guest introduced me to the Parable of the Pencil, and now I am going to introduce, or re-introduce it to you. The Pencil Maker took the pencil aside just before putting him into the box. "There are five things you need to know," he told the pencil, "before I send you out into the world. Always remember them and never forget, and you will become the best pencil you can be:

1. You will be able to do many great things, but only if you allow yourself to be held in someone's hand.

2. You will experience a painful sharpening from time to time, but you'll need it to become a better pencil.

3. You will be able to correct any mistakes you might make.

4. The most important part of you will always be what's inside.

5. On every surface you are used on, you must leave your mark. No matter what the condition, you must continue to write."

The pencil understood and promised to remember, and went into the box with purpose in its heart. Now replacing the place of the pencil with you, always remember those five points, and you will become the best person you can be.

1. You will be able to do many great things, but only if you allow yourself to be held in God's hand, and allow other human beings to access you for the many gifts you possess.

2. You will experience a painful sharpening from time to time by going through various problems, but you'll need it to become a stronger person.

3. You will be able to correct any mistakes you might make.

4. The most important part of you will always be what's on the inside.

5. On every surface you walk through, you must leave your mark. No matter what the situation, you must continue to do your duties. By understanding and remembering, proceed with your life on this earth, having a meaningful purpose in your heart.

Today's question: What lessons can you take away from the Parable of the Pencil?

What-Makes-You-Tick List

It is said that Beethoven at one point stopped writing for his generation, for most ignored, criticized or simply did not understand his music and what he was trying to do. He never stopped writing, however, but rather wrote for future audiences rather than his contemporaries. That is in some sense what I feel I am doing, especially with my book *Changing the Way We Do Church*. I consider that book one of my best. Most of the church doesn't get what I am writing, however, or if they do, it has had very little effect as far as I can tell. I am not whining, and I am open to the fact that maybe what I have to say isn't as good or relevant as I think it is. The other option is that it is for another time.

A colleague once posed a question in a staff devotion, and it gave me pause. The question was, "What makes you tick?" The answer to that question for Beethoven was to write cutting-edge music that had never been written before. One of the things that makes me tick is to see purpose impact people's lives, and then see that impact make a difference in the life of the local church. As I continued to answer my colleague's question, here is what I came up with:

1. Leadership development
2. Teaching/seminars/speaking
3. Writing
4. Broadcasting and publishing
5. Coaching—making room for others to do their thing
6. Travel to anywhere

7. Airports

8. Africa

9. Diversity involvement—working with people who don't look like me

10. Doing new things and creating order from their chaos

11. Reading/study/learning

12. Live events like plays and baseball games

13. Color—for example, I carry two bright orange pens with me everywhere I go

I wrote those things out in about five minutes. I then turned to two of my other colleagues and asked, "What makes you tick?" Neither one had a good answer if they had an answer at all. Now I will ask you: What makes you tick? Take five minutes and write down all the answers you can think of. Then carry that list with you for the next week and add to it as you encounter something else that makes you tick.

Your answers to that question are important, for you will end up doing what makes others tick if you don't face what motivates you. Once you have the list, don't do anything with it just yet. Simply study it and make sure it's complete. In the next chapter, we will create another list to help you understand what stops your clock.

WEEK
6

What-Stops-Your-Clock List

In the last chapter, I shared a list of things that make me tick. I hope you did the exercise I recommended to generate your own list. Now I want to share the "what stops my clock" list of those things that do not make me tick. It's just as important to identify what is on this list, for while the tick list can energize you, the what-stops-your-clock list will steal your energy and creativity like a bandit and never give any of it back. Here is my list. What's yours?

- Bureaucracy
- Authoritarian, arrogant leadership
- Traditions that don't make sense but carry the weight of law
- Hospital visitation
- Boring meetings
- Boring meetings that I have to attend and can't help make interesting
- People who don't ask me how I'm doing after I ask them
- Stingy people
- Lack of progress on a project
- Nepotism where the family member is not qualified for the position
- Bureaucracy (Oh, I already used that one, but it should count twice because I hate it so much)
- A class taught by a bad or poorly-prepared teacher

- Losing a game
- Self-absorbed leadership

As I study that list, I realize that most of those things involve people in one way or another, and some of them involve poor leadership. This shows me that I must be careful when I work with people, because they can take away my energy when they interfere with the task at hand. This list also shows me what my values are. If the things on my list demotivate me, then I must labor to make sure I am not guilty de-motivating others through the same behaviors or traits.

There you have my stop-my-clock list. Now, take five minutes and create yours. Don't spend a lot of time agonizing over it, but once you have it, study it to see what it reveals to you. Are you willing to build your life around the things that make you tick and minimize your encounters with the bandits? I hope you are.

Now that you have your two lists, study them both and see where you investing your time and effort – on things that make time fly or that cause it to drag on in boredom? As things emerge from your lists, begin to change engage activities that are more in line with who you are and what's most important to you.

Ask Yourself 100 Questions

You may not know your purpose because you don't ask enough good questions. If you are asking the right questions, you may not hold on to your unanswered questions until you find the answers, abandoning the quest. Finding and fulfilling your purpose can be hard work. There are few shortcuts and no easy or pat answers. Even when you discover purpose, it's often difficult to know how and where to invest yourself. In short, a PurposeQuest sometimes involves more heart and effort than a person is willing or able to give, and that may include you.

A well-known motivational speaker has stated that quality questions lead to a quality life. That pertains to your purpose, for you must proactively seek the truth concerning who you are, and part of that seeking is asking the right questions. My job, as a purpose coach and writer, is to equip you with those quality questions. After that, I have faith that the quality answers will come.

Let's look at an example of quality questions from the life of Nehemiah. Nehemiah was interested in Jerusalem and its residents, even though he had never been there. One day a group of travelers caught his attention as they discussed Jerusalem, and he asked them some questions. Their answers provoked him to prayer, thought and action. The rest is history as he found his purpose to go to Jerusalem and rebuild the ruined city. His mission started with good questions.

100 QUESTIONS

Once I was talking with my sister-in-law and the issue of asking good questions came up. She said those questions reminded her of a recommended exercise in a book I had given her by Michael Gelb entitled *How to Think Like Leonardo da Vinci*. Here is a recommendation that Gelb made:

> In your notebook, make a list of a hundred questions that are important to you. Your list can include any kind of question as long as it's something you deem significant: anything from "How can I save more money?" or "How can I have more fun?" to "What is the meaning and purpose of my existence?" and "How can I best serve the Creator?"
>
> Do the entire list in one sitting. Write quickly; don't worry about spelling, grammar, or repeating the same question in different words (recurring questions will alert you to emerging themes). Why a hundred questions? The first twenty or so will be "off the top of your head." In the next thirty or forty, themes often begin to emerge. And, in the latter part of the second half of the list, you are likely to discover unexpected but profound material.
>
> When you have finished, read through your list and highlight the themes that emerge. Consider the emerging themes without judging them. Are most of your questions about relationships? Business? Fun? Money? The meaning of life?

I came up with my hundred questions in about 30 minutes, so it doesn't take long. It was a valuable exercise that I have been processing for quite some time. Why not invest 30 minutes in your own questions that will help you discover your purpose. Then pick out a few questions and pursue them until you get an answer.

Strike the Waters

I have enjoyed my role as a college professor, and hope to do more and more teaching as the years go on. I love teaching new classes I have never taught before, because they direct me into areas of study that I would not ordinarily pursue. That causes me to grow. I recently completed my certification to conduct online classes, which is the wave od the future.

In a sense, I have been preparing for those classes all my life. I have diligently followed an aggressive reading and listening program for decades. I went back to school at age 57 to earn a Doctor of Ministry degree, and I have attended many seminars and certification classes. While I must prepare for each course, I am ready to teach because of my years of preparation. It makes me think of Elisha, who had traveled with Elijah and served him for many years. When Elijah was taken, Elisha took up the cloak Elijah had left behind and did what he had seen Elijah do:

> "Elisha then picked up Elijah's cloak that had fallen from him and went back and stood on the bank of the Jordan. He took the cloak that had fallen from Elijah and struck the water with it. 'Where now is the Lord, the God of Elijah?' he asked. When he struck the water, it divided to the right and to the left, and he crossed over" (2 Kings 2:13-14).

When I teach, I am striking the waters and, much to my ongoing amazement and joy, they part. God is helping me, even when I have not prepared as I desired for certain weeks. When that happens, a lifetime of preparation comes forth, and God does the rest—to God be the glory.

PERFECTIONISM

All this has delivered me from a desire for unrealistic perfectionism. I still pursue excellence, but I no longer define excellence as an absence of mistakes. I define it as a heart attitude that I will do my best with what I have and who I am, and trust the Lord for the rest. When I began my online Bible studies, I forced myself to send them out every week without proofing them. This made me uncomfortable, but I wanted to put the emphasis on creating the studies and not perfecting the studies.

Years later when I went back to edit those studies, I found the mistakes. In the nine years that I sent those weekly studies out, I never got an email or a comment drawing attention to the mistakes. Almost every week, however, I received emails of gratitude and appreciation for sending the studies. People shared what the studies meant to them, and I realized that my pursuit of perfection could have cost those people the help they received if I had not sent the studies out until they were "ready."

What about you? What are you preparing to do for the Lord that may take a few years or decades to complete? More importantly, when will you be ready to strike the waters like Elisha did and see the same results you watched others produce? Have you allowed your pursuit of perfection to prevent you from producing something that could honor God and help others?

Now may be the time for you to do what you have been talking about and preparing to do. Why not find a good situation to test the waters and see if God will act on your behalf because you have prepared for Him to do so? Don't put it off any longer. If you are not ready (and you may be more ready than you think you are), however, I urge you to get ready. Today I thank God I prepared for this day by His direction and grace, and I am having a wonderful time. God wants you to have the same experience. If I can help, let me know.

Disturb Me

During a recent seminar, I read a prayer I found in a book entitled *Chazown: A Different Way to See Your Life* by Craig Groeschel. I urge you to pray this prayer included below, if you dare. I already did and it works, but not in the way you may think.

DISTURB ME

The prayer was first prayed by Sir Francis Drake, who sailed around the world for England in 1577. The prayer goes like this:

> Disturb us, Lord, when we are too well pleased with ourselves, when our dreams have come true because we have dreamed too little, when we arrive safely because we have sailed too close to the shore.
>
> Disturb us, Lord, when with the abundance of things we possess, we have lost our thirst for the waters of life; having fallen in love with life, we have ceased to dream of eternity; and in our efforts to build a new earth, we have allowed our vision of the new Heaven to dim.
>
> Disturb us, Lord, to dare more boldly, to venture on wider seas where storms will show your mastery; where losing sight of land, we shall find the stars. We ask you to push back the horizons of our hopes; and to push into the future in strength, courage, hope, and love.

Now you see why I cautioned you about this dangerous prayer. As I travel and talk with people, however, it is a prayer that many desperately need to pray, and you may be among them.

SHRINKING BACK

Look at this passage found in Hebrews 10:35-39 that address the issues raised in the *Disturb Us* prayer:

> So do not throw away your confidence; it will be richly rewarded. You need to persevere so that when you have done the will of God, you will receive what he has promised. For in just a very little while, 'He who is coming will come and not delay. But my righteous one will live by faith. And if he shrinks back, I will not be pleased with him.' But we are not of those who shrink back and are destroyed, but of those who believe and are saved.

You may respond that you are living by faith, but perhaps that is because you are living so small. Your goals are timid, and your vision tiny because your fears have overwhelmed you. You are not doing anything beyond what you can see right in front of you, and to some it appears that you are living a busy life. Instead, you are living woefully below what God has for you. You have shrunk back to your comfort zone but describe it as only a place of respite, dreaming of what you will do one day when the conditions are just right.

I hope the previous paragraph doesn't describe your life. If it does, however, and you know it, now is the time to do something about it by setting some goals and living by faith once again. The beauty of doing this is that you don't need any idea of how you will accomplish those dreams; that's where the faith comes in. If you've decided, however, that faith is just too demanding or stressful, then you may be guilty of shrinking back, thus incurring God's displeasure.

Your choice is clear: have faith and please God, or shrink back and displease God. I hope you will choose wisely between the two. If you choose faith, then go back to the beginning of this chapter and pray the *Disturb Us* prayer every day this week. As you do, God will answer and will certainly disturb you with new visions and dreams before very long. Then you can set sail for destinations unknown, enjoying the journey as you venture onward in life.

Economic Terrorism

When you set out to fulfill your purpose, something interesting happens: you will be tested as to whether or not you can maintain purpose. Often this test is financial and involved what I refer to as financial terrorism. If the enemy of your soul can't keep you from purpose, he will try to surround your "city" and starve you into surrender, hoping you will give up and go back to your old job, your old way of life, your place of comfort. What's even more interesting is that God allows this to happen, for those tough times will equip you for your future success and keep you humble. This economic terrorism is a million-dollar experience that you would not give ten cents to go through again.

But you may ask: is there any biblical precedent for this terrorism" I believe there is. To see if you agree with me, you will have to read on.

THE LAND

God brought Abraham out of his homeland and promised to give him the land to which God was sending Him. He also promised that Abraham's descendants would be more numerous than the sands on the seashore. I wonder how Abraham knew about seashore sand, unless he had visited the beach during his lifetime? Anyway, I digress.

Abraham pursued his purpose and entered the land that God had promised. A curious thing happened, however, for at one point Abraham had to leave the very land God had given him. Why did he leave? The Bible tells us: "Now there was a famine in the land, and Abram went down to Egypt to live there for a while because the famine was severe" (Genesis 12:10).

21

God gave Abraham the land but then Abraham had to leave it because there was a famine and he would have starved! Why would God allow this to happen? One reason is so that God could reveal the work that still needed done in Abraham's' life and faith. This is evident when Abraham decided to misrepresent his wife Sarah, portraying her as his cousin and not his wife. That showed that Abraham's faith in the Lord was not where it needed to be for the ultimate fulfillment of his purpose. The other reason was to teach Abraham to hold on to God's promise and not look at the circumstances surrounding the promise.

Your own lack during your economic terrorism season will also reveal the real you, just like it did in Abraham's case.

MY OWN JOURNEY

I went through my own economic terrorism in 2001. There were days when I didn't think we were going to survive. I thought about turning aside to a job or some other means of support, but I decided to endure and press on. Years later, I am glad I did. What's more, my only regret is that I didn't engage my purpose earlier than 2001!

Today I am stronger and have more faith in God than ever before. I am not intimidated by my lack of resources as I set my goals. Famine, survival and economic terrorism taught me a lot about myself and God. I am a better servant of God today not only because of purpose, but because of my lack when I started to move forward.

Are you experiencing economic terrorism of some sort? This isn't an indication you have done something wrong, but something right! Don't panic, but instead, trust God. You will live, although there will be times when are you are convinced you won't! When it's over, you will be see what God was doing and has done, and you will rejoice. During the famine, it's difficult to do that.

If you are going through economic terrorism, use this time to strengthen your faith and keep your eyes on God. He is in control and won't allow your lack to last one day longer than it must. It must take place, however, and its end will bring not only a sigh of relief but also the great blessing that God had in mind as the end result all along.

Time Out, Time Off

I have been a college instructor since 1998. I enjoy being assigned classes to help fill out the semester course schedule because they help direct my study and help me grow. One semester I was asked to teach "The Theology of Paul from Romans to Timothy." While preparing for this class, I saw something about Paul I had never noticed.

TIME OUT

When Paul was at the peak of his ministry, he felt led to go to Jerusalem:

> "And now, compelled by the Spirit, I am going to Jerusalem, not knowing what will happen to me there. I only know that in every city the Holy Spirit warns me that prison and hardships are facing me. However, I consider my life worth nothing to me; my only aim is to finish the race and complete the task the Lord Jesus has given me—the task of testifying to the good news of God's grace" (Acts 20:22-24).

When Paul arrived in Jerusalem, he found that many in the city were ambivalent toward him and his ministry, so he made an effort to appease them by appearing in the Temple. This led to a near riot during which Paul was seized by the Roman guards to save his life. From there he went to Caesarea to stand trial and eventually appealed to Caesar, which took him to Rome, a place he had desired to visit for some time.

It was a four-year period from the time that Paul arrived in Jerusalem until the end of the book of Acts when he was under house arrest in Rome. And that is the point that made an impression on me. At the time when Paul was most knowledgeable and experienced, when he could have been so productive traveling to strengthen the churches and disciples, God took Paul out of circulation for four years.

TIME OFF

Why would God do this? I am not second guessing the Lord, for He knew what He was doing during this period of Paul's life. Yet let's examine those four years from Paul's perspective. Paul had done so much for so long and then he was forced to take a time out. During those years, his enemies were free to move into the churches he planted to distort Paul's gospel. Paul could do nothing but trust God and the people who had served his ministry to sort out the problems.

It was during these four years that Paul wrote what are known as his prison epistles—Ephesians, Philippians, Colossians and Philemon. To write with the insight Paul had, he needed time to reflect on his message and think. He could not produce fresh material and do what he had been doing as an itinerate preacher. God had him take some time off through a time out, and the results were letters that still impact the world today. Paul had to let go of his today in order to embrace his tomorrow. Oh yes, and suffering played a big part in this four-year season of personal growth and development.

Maybe that's where you are. If God has used you, He may be giving you time off in order to sharpen and freshen your perspective. It's not easy to go from busy to full stop, but those seasons help define who you are and the legacy you will leave. Don't fight it, no matter how difficult the time out may be. Instead make the most of your time off from being in charge and busy. In sports, every time out ends with play being resumed, and the same will be true for you.

Self-Promotion 1

I had an interesting chat on Facebook with a friend who was in turmoil. He is talented and gifted, but struggles when it comes to what he called "self-promotion." He asked me how, after a lifetime of being taught that any kind of promoting self is wrong, how he could step forward and talk about himself, his gifts and what God has put in his heart to do?

That's a great question and one that I have pondered for a long time. It has been an interesting dynamic that people are happy that I write books. Those same people are unhappy when I try to sell them, deeming my efforts shameless self promotion. Why wouldn't I tell people I have a book that can help them with the specific issue that is addressed in the book? In the minds of some, that's just plain wrong.

CONCEIT

The main concern with self-promotion is best summarized in Philippians 2:3, where Paul wrote: "Do nothing out of selfish ambition or vain conceit. Rather, in humility value others above yourselves." Many conclude after reading this verse that talking about yourself in almost any situation is wrong or at least improper, and ambition is considered to be in bad taste or downright evil. Are these interpretations correct?

Here are some thoughts off the top of my head for this discussion:

1. When Paul wrote his letters, he clearly identified himself as an apostle.

2. David approached Goliath and declared what he was going to do to the giant in no uncertain terms.

3. Jesus made many claims, although sometimes veiled to hide from unbelievers, concerning who He was and what He had come to do

Let's examine that last point a little more.

A PUBLIC FIGURE

Jesus' family thought he was self-promoting and eager to be a public figure as you can see from John 7:3-4: "Jesus' brothers said to him, 'Leave Galilee and go to Judea, so that your disciples there may see the works you do. No one who wants to become a public figure acts in secret. Since you are doing these things, show yourself to the world.'" It's comforting to know that Jesus' family thought He was self-promoting. To some extent they were correct. He was promoting, but with a purpose. Is that possible for you and I to do the same?

When you consider it, weren't Jesus' miracles a means by which He could gather a crowd to announce the coming of His kingdom? Did not the Father make Jesus a household name and a celebrity in all of Israel? Did Jesus gather disciples whom He then sent out to extend His work and announce God's plan with even greater fervor and success than He did?

We are not going to settle this issue in this chapter, but I wanted to start the dialogue with these thoughts. What do you think? Is it wrong to promote yourself? When, if ever, is it permissible? Does Philippians 2:3 prohibit any kind of ambition or marketing? I leave you to ponder these questions until you read the next chapter.

Self-Promotion 2

The issue before us is this: What is self-promotion and is it inappropriate to engage in it? There are some who look with disfavor and even disdain on anyone or any ministry that is involved in what they consider self-promoting activities. Are they correct? Does the Bible forbid self-promotion? Let's continue our discussion of this misunderstood concept.

YOUR LIGHT

My thoughts for this chapter come from Matthew 5:14-16, where it says to do your deeds so others can see:

> "You are the light of the world. A town built on a hill cannot be hidden. Neither do people light a lamp and put it under a bowl. Instead they put it on its stand, and it gives light to everyone in the house. In the same way, let your light shine before others, that they may see your good deeds and glorify your Father in heaven."

Later in the same sermon, Jesus gave this warning:

> "Be careful not to practice your righteousness in front of others to be seen by them. If you do, you will have no reward from your Father in heaven. So when you give to the needy, do not announce it with trumpets . . ." (Matthew 6:1-2).

Here we have an important distinction between selfish and godly self-promotion. On the one hand, we are not to parade our righteous acts, such as giving alms, which will glorify self. On the other hand, we are to do our good deeds in such a way that others will see them and glorify God.

Since God has given you your gifts and purpose that enables you to do your good deeds, then I conclude that, in most cases, it is permissible to let people know what you can do, when God enables and empowers you to do it. For example, I am a gifted event coordinator and administrator. I am also a quick and efficient writer. I sense God helping me when I do those things and the feedback over the years has been positive.

Is it wrong to tell others about those gifts? If they need an event planned or some administrative help, have I sinned if I advertise my abilities so others know that I can effectively serve them in those particular areas?

SERVICE

What's more, if God has given you gifts and a purpose to be used to help others, then isn't letting people know what you can to serve them consistent with letting your light shine as we read above? 1 Peter 4:10 states, "Each of you should use whatever gift you have received to serve others, as faithful stewards of God's grace in its various forms." When I write a book, am I permitted to tell others that I have written it? Can I set up a book table to sell those books or even to give them away? Is it self-promoting when I honestly feel what I have written can help the reader, and therefore I want them to know that the book exists?

It probably is selfish self-promotion if I tattoo the name of my book to my right hand to make sure everyone sees it. It is selfish if I shift every conversation to a discussion of what I can do. If my self-promotion is solely for the purpose of making money or advancing my career, then I have stepped over the line. If my intent is right, however, and I want to serve others with the gifts God has given me, then it seems that I am not engaging in self-promotion but rather God-promotion.

Paul seemed content with those who were doing good work for the wrong reason. In Philippians he penned this amazing statement:

It is true that some preach Christ out of envy and rivalry, but others out of goodwill. The latter do so out of love, knowing that I am put here for the defense of the gospel. The former preach Christ out of selfish ambition, not sincerely, supposing that they can stir up trouble for me while I am in chains. But what does it matter? The important thing is that in every way, whether from false motives or true, Christ is preached. And because of this I rejoice (Philippians 1:15-18).

It seems that some people were preaching Christ out of rivalry with other ministries, promoting themselves as they preached the gospel. How did Paul deal with that fact? He rejoiced because he knew God could use those all-too-human motives to accomplish His purposes.

Let's continue our discussion in the next two chapters, for it's important for you to come to grips with when to self-promote and when to fall back.

Self-Promotion 3

Let's continue our discussion of self-promotion trying to determine what it is and if it permissible under any circumstances for a believer.

MAGNIFY THE LORD

In the Old Testament, we are told to magnify the Lord. We have made that simply a matter of praise and worship where we exalt and describe God's attributes in clear and exuberant musical expressions. Stop and think about that word "magnify." Doesn't it also mean to take the smallest thing and make it larger so it is easier to see and examine? Could it mean that we are to take the smallest thing that God has done through us and in us and make it *bigger* for all to see, not with the intent to see us, but in seeing us to help others see Him?

Is self-promotion, done with right intent, really any different than giving a testimony? When God does something for you—provides, heals, delivers or reveals—is it wrong to stand up and say what He has done? So if God has given you a gift or purpose, is it any different to broadcast the truth of what God has done in and through you? And when you do, is that not the same as magnifying the Lord—taking His work in you and "blowing it up" for all the world to see.

INTENT

Self-promotion can come from two sources: the selfish desire to promote yourself, or the desire to further God's work through you as you serve others. Consider what Paul said in Romans 11:13-14 (NKJV): "For I speak to you Gentiles; inasmuch as I am an apostle to the Gentiles, I magnify my ministry, if by any means I may provoke to jealousy those who are my flesh and save some of them."

In the NKJV, it states that Paul magnified his office. Other translations of that verse render it "proud of, make as much as I can of, glorify my ministry." Paul magnified his ministry so he could win more Jews to the gospel. Paul promoted what he did because God appointed him and Paul knew that his work was the most important work in the world. He was not concerned with what others thought, only what God thought. Paul was telling the truth with the right motives, and therefore he magnified himself so he could ultimately magnify the Lord.

Your job is not just to magnify the Lord by behaving and not robbing banks or watching bad movies. Even nonbelievers do those things. What they cannot do that you can is to express God's love to His creation, specifically through your purpose, gifts and goals. Perhaps it is time you faced the fact that your distaste for what you call self-promotion is really a means to protect yourself from criticism and being misunderstood. Jesus and Paul "promoted" and were criticized; can you expect any different treatment?

Self-Promotion 4

We have been discussing the delicate and sensitive issue of self promotion, trying to determine if and when it is ever appropriate for believers to draw attention to themselves. There are some that oppose this concept under any conditions and then there are others who have no problem "tooting their own horn" every chance they get. Let's wrap up our discussion in this chapter.

THE CHRISTMAS STAR

It seems to me that the star the Magi followed was a publicity gimmick of sorts. It appeared to announce the birth and location of Jesus the Messiah. It seems that the only ones who saw it were some men from the East, and even Matthew is the only gospel writer who tells the star story:

> After Jesus was born in Bethlehem in Judea, during the time of King Herod, Magi from the east came to Jerusalem and asked, "Where is the one who has been born king of the Jews? We saw his star when it rose and have come to worship him" (Matthew 2:1-2).

> After they had heard the king, they went on their way, and the star they had seen when it rose went ahead of them until it stopped over the place where the child was. When they saw the star, they were overjoyed. On coming to the house, they saw the child with his mother Mary, and they bowed down and worshiped him. Then they opened their treasures and presented him with gifts of gold, frankincense and myrrh (Matthew 2:9-11).

The star was precise and allowed the men to prepare in advance for their journey by bringing gifts. There were many other events that served to promote the birth of Jesus, but this one is special. All the other events came to people who were passive and not involved in obtaining the promotions—the shepherds were at work when the angels appeared and God sovereignly chose Mary and Joseph (they had not been seeking any role in the Christmas story).

The Magi were different because they were *looking* for the star and then travelled probably hundreds of miles at great personal expense and discomfort to find what the star was promoting. When I pondered this, I saw self-promotion in a whole different light, pardon the pun.

THE SEEKERS

The star came for those who had need, who were diligently searching for that star. Someone had told the Magi that a King would be born, and they and their ancestors had searched to find who He was for centuries. They had faith and they had need, for they came not only to honor the King but also to worship Him. They were hungry for the things of God and God sent a promotional star just for them. Perhaps other saw it, but no one else followed it but these Magi.

You should self-promote not for your benefit but for the benefit of those who are seeking who you are, what you have, and what you can do. If you can pray and people are healed, then healed people need you by the will of the Lord who gave you the gift of healing. If you can write, then you let others know you can, for someone is out there searching for a "star," something to lead them to what they were seeking to find.

If you have died in Christ and belong to Him, then your gift, purpose and role in society are not your choice or call. If God wants to make you a household name, it's none of your business. There are some members of the body who are created to be behind the scenes, but there are some who are made to be seen. Into whichever category you fall, your life is not your own. It belongs to God and others.

Let's get over any vestiges of false humility that say, "If God or anyone needs me, they can come find me. I am not going to help them by self-promoting, for that is not spiritual or proper." If that's how you think, I advise you to "get over it!" and allow all those who need to see your star do that so they know where you live so they can find the help they need that can only come from you. Then they will do just what the Magi did—they will worship *Him*, not you—and that is exactly where your self-promoting activities should lead.

I Learned to Speak by Not Speaking

It may sound like a paradox when I write that I learned to speak by *not* speaking. After all, isn't the essence of public speaking someone standing in front of a crowd and sharing thoughts or lessons? How can anyone learn how to do something by not doing it? Let's examine those questions more carefully and see if we can come up some answers that make sense.

ELEVEN YEARS

I was an associate pastor for 11 years from 1978-1989. While I had many chances to lead a small home group, I only got two chances in those 11 years to speak before the entire church. The second time I spoke was the last Sunday before I left, so it's an accurate statement that I averaged one talk every 11 years. That's a lot of preparation time between messages, don't you think?

What did I do all those 600 Sundays, plus conferences and special meetings, when I watched and listened to countless other speakers? I got ready to speak!

I knew that one day I would address large audiences, even though I was far from doing that during those 11 years. First, I would visualize myself speaking before people. I tell audiences today that I saw them *before* I ever came to be with them. Second, I studied the speakers I witnessed. I watched what worked and what didn't work when they spoke. I fashioned in my mind what kind of speaker I would be before I ever got a chance to speak, just by watching and learning. The most difficult thing during those years was to watch ineffective speakers when I knew in my heart that I could do a better job.

Third, I prepared things to say, even though I had no invitations or speaking engagements at which to say them. I created the *Life is a Gold Mine* seminar in 1985, well before I ever had an invitation to deliver it. I prepared the slides, outlines and material. I had a few chances outside of my local church to speak, and I made the most of those opportunities, although at times I wasn't very effective.

Finally, I never gave up my dream, even though I had few opportunities to speak. I watched comediennes, listened and read great speeches of history, and went to school to earn a doctorate. I did all I knew to do. There were times I was so discouraged when nothing happened to advance my vision that I wept with sadness—but I *never* gave up.

THE BREAKTHROUGH

Then I moved to Orlando in 1989 to pastor a church, at which time I also began to speak in jails and prisons. I spoke once a week at the church, but often spoke six or seven times a week to men and women behind bars. I went from not speaking to nonstop speaking. Today, I have no lack of speaking engagements, and I continue to hone my skills. My main preparation, however, was during those 11 years of non-activity.

What is the lesson here that is important for you to grasp? It's found in Proverbs 22:29: "Do you see a man skilled in his work? He will serve before kings; he will not serve before obscure men."

I don't care what your dream is. If you spend time pursuing excellence and becoming good at what you do, you won't have to go looking for "kings." The kings will come looking for you. Don't waste any more time waiting for your breakthrough or trying to make something happen. Instead, invest your time in preparing for the day when your breakthrough comes, and that preparation can begin the minute you finish reading this chapter.

Fighting Yourself

You are probably familiar with what Jesus said in John 7:38: "Whoever believes in me, as the Scripture has said, streams of living water will flow from within him." When you believe in Jesus, there is a flow that emanates from you and the water from that flow, while originating in the Spirit, should taste like you. It is comprised of your gifts, personality, the expressions of your life's work, your values, life philosophy and worldview. The flow can't be bitter with anger or unforgiveness, and it can't be salty with lies and deception. It should also not be artificially flavored to taste like someone else's water. Other than that, the water should taste like you.

This is important because you may be among the many who believe that your water is "bad." If it isn't bad, you may think it needs to have another flavor or maybe some fizzy gas added. Many people are fighting themselves, who they are and what they like, even trying to distance themselves from the dreams in their hearts. If that's you, can you recognize how counterproductive it is for you to be opposing yourself?

YOUR FLAVOR

I love live sporting events. I make people laugh. I thrive when I travel and am bored with the mundane. I love teaching, and dread bureaucracy. I love to write and sign books, even shaking hands and posing for a picture or two with my "fans." That is who I am and what my water tastes like. My writing, speaking and consulting has my "flavor," and it flows out of me freely. That water tastes like purpose, productivity, goal setting and being true to yourself. Can you describe to me the flavor of your living water?

Are you filtering the water for impurities and then letting it gush from your life? Or are you damming up the flow, trying not to be who you are? Keep in mind, the water that flows is not for your benefit; it's for others to drink. In this case, it's alright for people to flavor their water to taste like yours, until they can develop their own.

Is there anything you enjoy doing or being that you are trying to curtail or adjust? Maybe those characteristics or interests are part of your flow and you should stop interfering with their expression. Perhaps a characteristic that you are convinced has to change is something God built into you. When you oppose it, you are actually opposing God, telling Him He made a mistake when He put that in you.

Based on this truth, I will continue to smile and shake hands as I go, not worrying about why I enjoy it as much as I do. I want to be who God made me to be and if anyone has a problem with that, it is their problem and not mine. At one point in my life, I tired of opposing myself and I hope you get tired of opposing yourself, too.

Exiled

I have taught a course called "Apocalyptic Literature" on several occasions, and it is always a challenge because of the preconceived ideas the students have. I focus the class on John's Revelation, but have also looked at apocalyptic sections in Daniel and Ezekiel. One thing that struck me about all of those authors is that they were in exile when they received their revelation. John was on Patmos and the other two were in Babylon. I thought it interesting that they were all in foreign lands when they received a coded message from heavenly headquarters revealing important truth. That insight led me to reflect on my own exile and the role it played in my personal development and life message. Let me explain.

EXILED

In 2001, I made a major life and ministry transition. I went from the phone ringing off the hook to no one calling. My calendar, once chock full to overflowing, was empty. People called me *not* to come visit them, but rather to stay away. The only door that was open to me, with a few exceptions, was in Africa. I have always said that God will make His will clear by eliminating all other options. I knew without a doubt Africa was where I was to spend my time.

When I started to travel there, I went for two weeks at a time. Then I expanded it to four, then eight and then at times up to 14 to 16 weeks. When I add up all the time I spent in Africa from 2001 to 2009, it came to a total of 4.5 years. I refer to that time as my exile.

There were days and nights during my exile where no one knew where I was but the Lord. I wasn't imprisoned during those years, but I was in a place where I was pretty much alone and had lots of time to think, write and reflect. Those years represent a million-dollar experience that I would not give you ten cents to go through again. It was valuable but painful, priceless but costly, and I learned a lot about myself in those years.

Some of what I learned was what I had to unlearn, for there were attitudes and habits that were not appropriate for what the Lord had in store for me in the coming years.

PURPOSE

God had a purpose for my exile, just like He did for John, Daniel and Ezekiel. Sometimes you must have a radical break from your routine in order for God to reveal Himself to you in new ways. He needs to take you out of your comfort zone to new levels of intimacy and insight, and that can only happen when it's you and Him and very few others. Exile is painful, but it is also critical if you are to reach your full potential.

Like the three apocalyptic authors, I too gained much insight from my exile. I faced and embraced my creativity during my exile. It is when I confronted negative thinking that was limiting God's work in my life. It was also when I learned to trust Him for more than ever before.

God has a purpose for your exile, too. You may find yourself alone or out of the loops that were once an integral part of your life. You haven't done anything wrong, but God has to take you away from life as you have known it to speak to you and work on some things. The three exiled authors were all productive in their exile. What's more, they received and wrote about things that still impact the world today. God knew what He was doing with them, He knew what He was doing with me and He knows what He is doing with you. Trust Him.

Don't only trust Him, however, but make your exile a development time that will serve you well in the coming years. Learn, study, grow, try new things, make new friends but most of all plumb the depths of God's love and purpose for you. When your exile ends, and it almost always ends, you will be a new and better version of your old self, and who knows what revelation you will receive during that time. For while all others may forsake you, God never will, and that is the most important thing to know about exile. Before you had to share your time with others; in exile you have all the time in the world for God. Make the most of it and have faith that your exile will eventually end and you will be able to come "home" once again.

Anointed Ignorance

In my career as a college instructor, I have taught 34 different undergraduate classes and nine graduate courses. The usual philosophy is for an instructor to focus on one area or topic, so that the professor can continue to build on his or her expertise. That ensures that the students are getting the best the professors have to offer in their area of interest and emphasis.

Just so you don't misunderstand, I am not teaching physics or astronomy, subjects for which I know nothing about. My course subjects are in the areas of theology, biblical studies, and practical church issues. When I teach classes for the first time, I am forced to learn new things. What's more, I am less of an expert, encouraging the students to learn along with me, and our educational journey is much more rewarding when I can create that atmosphere of learning.

These new courses serve one other purpose in my life: Without them and what they force me to do, all I have is anointed ignorance. Let me explain what that term means.

AN EXAMPLE

If God pours out His Spirit on me (or you), we have some measure of anointing. Yet if I am ignorant (not stupid, just ignorant—capable but undeveloped), then I have God's anointing, but He doesn't have very much to anoint. Therefore, I have anointed ignorance. I have His Spirit, but I don't have the necessary knowledge or wisdom to go with it.

Here's an example. Perhaps you are talking with someone and you think of a verse of Scripture that could help them at that point in time. The problem is that you don't have your

Bible with you. You have the desire to help, perhaps even the anointing to help, but you don't have the knowledge to help. You have anointed ignorance.

Now let's say that you had taken the time and made the effort to memorize that passage. Now when you are talking to a person and the "anointing" is present, the knowledge is also present and you can share that passage, even though you don't have your Bible.

THERE'S MORE

In addition to all this, recent studies prove that your brain never gets old and wears out. It maintains its ability to learn and develop new habits and thinking patterns all your life, barring some disease or trauma. Therefore, you can keep confronting your areas of ignorance by continuing to learn and grow mentally and intellectually, thus increasing your usefulness to God and His people.

I went back to school later in life than many typically do and I now teach as often as I can because I still have a lot of ignorance. The only way to rectify that is to learn and then offer my learning to God so that He can use it for His purpose and glory. What's more, God does not promote potential; He promotes people who have developed their potential, those who have confronted their ignorance in the midst of their anointing.

Are you waiting for God to promote you *before* you have developed yourself and the potential He gave you? Are you asking the Lord to do all He can do while you are not prepared to do all you can do? I urge you to do something to address and develop your potential. Otherwise, you will be stuck with a whole lot of anointed ignorance, which can only be addressed when you take the time and make the effort to fill the void where ignorance resides.

The Old Folks Were Right

When I was younger, I would ask some older folks in church, "How are you doing?" They would sometimes answer, "I got up this morning, so I am fine." I remember thinking, "That's kind of simplistic, and it didn't tell me how they were doing." Now I am in my sixties and have witnessed the burial some of my older and younger friends and peers. When I arise in the morning, I find myself thanking God that He gave me another day. Suddenly what those older folks had to say doesn't sound so strange.

In fact, when I get up these days, I have a litany of things for which I give thanks. I won't go into them here, but with age comes the realization of and appreciation for both what the Lord has done in my life and His gift of another day of life. I meditate on what the psalmist wrote: "Teach us to *number* our days, that we may gain a heart of wisdom" (Psalm 90:12. emphasis added). I don't know how many days I have left, but let's assume I live to be my mother's age of 92. That means I have about 10,000 days left. If I live to be my father's age, I have about 6,000 left. While either option would be nice, for all I know I may only have one day remaining, so I want to make the most of each one of them, whether one or 10,000.

THE QUOTE

Pablo Picasso, the great painter, once said, "Only put off until tomorrow what you are willing to die having left undone." While I am thankful for today, I want to make the most of it by doing what I can with what I have. I want to run as fast, as far and as long as I can, and if that is a month longer or 30 years, I am already thankful for whatever opportunities the Lord gives me.

When I served as a pastor, I presided over enough funerals to let me know that the old die, and the young can die. No one is getting out of here alive, and all of our days are numbered. When I hear people talk about what they will do "one day," I commend them for planning ahead. I also urge them to act with urgency, for that "one day" may be sooner than they think. When I come to the Christmas holiday season, I keep in mind that it could be my last one, so I make the most of it, enjoying every day with those whom I love.

I write with that attitude and I travel to where I want to go now because I am not guaranteed the future. I am grateful for the days I have, and I want to make the most of them. Those older folks taught me to be thankful for every day, recognizing it as the gift that it is—you should do the same. Then once you have started your day with thanks, I want you to aggressively embrace the days you have left—to number them as the psalmist wrote—so you will have a heart of wisdom.

Succcccess

My computer spell check is trying to tell me I misspelled succcccess. I spelled it like that on purpose, however, because I want to start a series that focuses on the five c's in succcccess. Since success only has two C's, I thought I would add three more for affect. Each of the five begins with the letter C, thus necessitating the change in spelling.

THE FIRST THREE

Not too long ago I taught a class for a special program of college graduates called "A Love and Theology for the City." In one session, we were discussing with the students what it takes to launch and sustain succcccessful initiatives in poor areas. The more we discussed it, the clearer it was to me that what it takes to succcccceed in urban work and ministry is the same as what it takes to be succcccessful in any other area as well. Armed with that conclusion, let's dive into the first three c's.

1. *Curiosity*. If you want to know where to start in your quest for purposeful succcccess, start with your curiosity. Answer the question, "What interests you?" and then pursue the answers. As you do, you may try to "figure out" how you can make money from that interest and, if you can't see how, you will abandon your interests. Don't think like that. Follow your interests and see where they lead you. God can take some of the simplest interests and help you turn them into a business, organization, movement or project that will bless or edify others.

2. *Creativity*. I have written extensively on creativity and you can read some of what I have written on my website.

Suffice it to say that you were created by the Creator in His image, which is to be creative. There is no end of your ability to be creative as you express your life experience as seen through your eyes. Adam named all the animals in the Garden and he used his God-given creativity to do so. What assignment has God given you that requires you to do the same?

3. *Competence.* God does not promote people with potential. He promotes those who have developed their potential. You need to become the best you that you can be, and that will require work, training, education, apprenticeship, coaching, spiritual disciplines and godliness. There are no shortcuts to growth and personal development, so don't even look for them. There is only one way to develop yourself and that is to invest time, money and effort into becoming more effective tomorrow than you are today.

THE LAST TWO

Now let's look at the last two c's in succcccess.

4. *Collaboration.* You will need to team and partner with other people if you are going to make a major impact through your life's work. You can't do it all. Rather you must do what you do best and team with others who do what they do best that contributes to the overall effort. What's more, you must know your own strengths and weaknesses, and understand how your personality and characteristics will best mesh (or cause some friction) with others.

5. *Commitment.* You will be tested in your resolve to finish the task at hand. God will use your failures and setbacks to conform you to Christ's image. If you faint in the heat of the day, you will not be able to achieve your dreams or fulfill your purpose. Winston Churchill once addressed an audience of youth, said, "Never, never, never, never, never give up," and then sat down. That's all he had to say, but it was great advice. As long as you have breath, stay the course.

There you have the five key elements that lead to succcccess. We will take a closer look at each one over the next five chapters and learn how to develop and apply them in your life's work. I have not included any Bible verses in this chapter, but don't worry, there will be plenty in the chapters to come.

Curiosity

In the last chapter, I explained that we are going to be looking at five concepts that all being with the letter C that help spell *succcccess*. I promised to touch on each one of the five in more depth in the coming chapters, so here is the follow up to that promise. I have actually thought of several more c's since last week, but I am not ready to expand the series, otherwise I will have to spell success "succcccccccccccess." Maybe that would not be such a bad thing, but for now, let's dive into the concept of curiosity and learn how it relates to succcccess.

A BURNING BUSH

We know that Moses tended sheep in the wilderness for forty years! I have been to the Middle East numerous times and it is a hot place. Moses had to work in this heat year in and year out, and I am sure that every now and then a dry bush would burst into flames due to the super-hot conditions. Then one day Moses saw something unusual that captured his attention:

> Now Moses was tending the flock of Jethro his father-in-law, the priest of Midian, and he led the flock to the far side of the wilderness and came to Horeb, the mountain of God. There the angel of the Lord appeared to him in flames of fire from within a bush. Moses saw that though the bush was on fire it did not burn up. So Moses thought, "I will go over and see this strange sight—why the bush does not burn up" (Exodus 3:1-3).

What was unusual about this bush is that it burned, probably a common sight, but the bush was not consumed. It

49

just kept on burning. Moses could have easily dismissed this sight and went about his business, but he decided to investigate further. Upon closer examination, he had a surprising thing happen: "When the Lord saw that he had gone over to look, God called to him from within the bush, "Moses! Moses!" And Moses said, "Here I am" (Exodus 3:4).

SO WHAT?

Moses did not approach the bush because God called him. It was his curiosity that caused Moses to pause and look, and only then did God call out to Moses and initiate a series of events that changed the course of history. In this order of events, first came Moses' curiosity, then his reaction, God's call and finally, Moses' response to God. What does this have to do with your succccess?

There are many people waiting for God's call. Perhaps you are one of them. Did you ever consider that the call may be in what interests you? You are probably busy and don't see how what interests you can add to your career. Therefore, you don't pursue what is in your heart. Because you don't respond to what is in you, you go about your business and wonder why God is not answering your prayers to be used or promoted.

It was the apostle Paul's interest, his obsession with persecuting Christians, that led him to be a Christian and become the apostle Paul. If God can use Saul's misdirected interest to direct his steps, then God can use your curiosities to do the same. Succcccess starts with investigating what piques your interest. Do something to satisfy your curiosity this week. Read a book, go to a museum, have lunch with a colleague, or draw a picture.

Don't try to figure out why you are doing it, or what good it will contribute in the long run. Approach it like Moses did the bush or Paul went after the Christians. As you do it, however, listen for God's voice, that may be something as subtle as, "I like this and think I will do it again." That's how you follow your curiosity until it becomes a passion.

Creativity

In the last chapter, we began a discussion of the five c's in succcccess. If you think succcccess should not be a consideration for you, read these words from Psalm 1:1-3 in the Good News Translation:

> "Happy are those who reject the advice of evil people, who do not follow the example of sinners or join those who have no use for God. Instead, they find joy in obeying the Law of the Lord, and they study it day and night. They are like trees that grow beside a stream, that bear fruit at the right time, and whose leaves do not dry up. *They succeed in everything they do*" (emphasis added).

With that in mind, let's look at the second c in succcccess, that being creativity.

YES, YOU ARE!

In 2006, I had a startling revelation and changed my purpose statement from "I *bring* order out of chaos" to "I *create* order out of chaos." It was then that I accepted the fact that I am a creative person, something I had denied up to that point. I began to write and teach about creativity after that, and I have many *articles* on my website devoted to the subject of creativity.

I also have a list of creative expressions sent to me by my readers over the years after they read some of my material. They listed child raising, letter writing, problem solving, public speaking, and time management as activities people engage in every day that require creativity. This is valuable to understand, because most people consider only artists or poets as creative. If you have children or manage your time, however, you are creative, too!

CREATIVITY FOLLOWS CURIOSITY

In the last chapter, we looked at the first c in succcccess and that is curiosity. Once you are curious and decide to follow your heart and what interests you, it is time to express your creativity. You can then begin to structure your world and invest your time in such a way that your creativity can take shape as a practical expression of who you are. I am interested in writing, and have been since I was young. So in 1995 at the age of 45, I started to pursue my interest and today I write every day to an audience all over the world.

I have written 75 books, edited many others, composed more than 1,000 *Monday Memos*, finished a verse-by-verse devotional on the entire New Testament, and wrote a daily devotional online for seven years. Currently I am teaching four college classes and have numerous other creative projects and ideas in the works. I love to do media but got tired of waiting for people to invite me to be part of their media world. Therefore, I started my own online shows and at one time hosted five weekly broadcasts.

You don't have to do any of those things that I am doing to be creative. You simply have to be yourself. You cannot be fighting yourself, however, and be creative. My experience is that many people (perhaps even you) are trying to talk themselves out of their creativity instead of into it. With that in mind, I encourage you to read my past *Memos*, think about this in the coming days and embrace your creativity. You cannot be succcccessful without employing your creativity, but you cannot employ it if you deny that it even exists.

It will help you to sit down and in ten minutes list all the creative expressions you have in your life. Once you see and accept that you are creative, your life will change, as mine did, and your creative expressions will leap from your heart and mind into a world that is waiting for them to appear. Have fun, and be creative!

Competence

In this chapter, let's continue our discussion of the five c's in succccccess with the third c, competence. Let me say at the start that God does not promote or use people with potential. He does not promote holy people simply because they are holy. God promotes and uses holy people who have developed their potential through competence and fruitfulness. Don't believe that? Then read on and see if I can convince you.

PROOF PLEASE

Here are some statements about the importance of competence for you to consider:

1. Daniel — Daniel served with distinction in Babylon. He was promoted because of his gifts that God gave him, but he developed them, as it was said of Daniel: "At this, the administrators and the satraps tried to find grounds for charges against Daniel in his conduct of government affairs, but they were unable to do so. They could find no corruption in him, because he was trustworthy and neither corrupt nor negligent" (Daniel 6:4). Daniel was a great administrator.

2. David — David was a prolific songwriter and poet who honed his skills through regular use. He was also a magnificent warrior and leader, of whom the people sang: "When the men were returning home after David had killed the Philistine, the women came out from all the towns of Israel to meet King Saul with singing and dancing, with joyful songs and with timbrels and lyres. As they danced, they sang: "Saul has slain his thousands, and David his tens of thousands" (1 Samuel 18:6-7).

3. Esther — Esther was a beautiful woman, by God's

design: "This young woman, who was also known as Esther, had a lovely figure and was beautiful" (Esther 2:7b). What did God do with her beauty? He dispatched her to the king's servants, who bestowed beauty treatments on Esther for one year. The result: She was even more beautiful than before!

4. Paul—Paul knew four languages and was from one of the most cross-cultural city in the Roman Empire. He was a Jew of Jews and a perfect keeper of God's law by his own admission: ". . . as for righteousness based on the law, faultless" (Philippians 3:6). What did God do with this man who had excelled in Judaism? He chose Paul to be His representative to the Gentiles. God took Paul's skill, redirected and perfected it, and used it for His glory.

THE LESSON FOR YOU

The lesson for you should be clear. God uses you to the extent that you have developed your skills and gifts. If you are competent, He will use you. If you are competent and have integrity, He will promote you to the highest levels that your gifts and foundation will allow you to attain. Your succcccess in any field or endeavor is a partnership with God, who provides the grace and opportunities, and you, who develop your competence.

What is your plan for competence? Do you even have one? In what field or effort do you want to be competent, even world-class, in skill and effect? Mind you, I am not suggesting that competence is more important than holiness or integrity. I am saying, however, that without competence your holiness alone will limit God's ability to use you to the fullest extent of your potential. Give some thought this week to the importance of competence in succcccess and then go about a one-year, five-year or lifetime plan to achieve the greatest skill possible for you as you express your purpose and pursue your goals.

Collaboration

We are almost finished with our discussion of the five c's in succcccess. So far, we have covered Curiosity, Creativity, and Competence. In this chapter, let's take a look at collaboration.

YAY TEAM!

God did not create you with the capability to do everything, just certain things. If you could do it all, you would not have need of anyone else. The same is true for organizations. Even large corporations need to collaborate with others or else build an organization big enough so that everything they need is under one corporate umbrella. In a sense, they are then collaborating within their organization, but still must at times build partnerships with other entities.

Here are a few examples of teams working together in the Bible:

1. Joseph and Pharaoh made a great team in Egypt, with Joseph providing the administration and Pharaoh the leadership.

2. Moses and Aaron led the Israelites out of Egypt.

3. Saul and David enjoyed success early in their partnership as they defeated the Philistines again and again.

4. Nehemiah partnered with the king he served to secure permission and resources to rebuild Jerusalem.

5. Daniel had three friends who served with him in Babylon.

6. Jesus had twelve disciples with whom he collaborated and worked closely.

7. Barnabas and Saul, Paul and Silas, Paul and Luke, and a number of other combinations worked together to spread the gospel to the Gentiles in the early church.

I hope you are taking in the idea which is you are going to be succcccessful, you need to collaborate and partner with others, whether you are looking for individual or corporate succcccess.

SOME SUGGESTIONS

Here are some suggestions to enable you to collaborate effectively:

1. *Find those who share your values and ethics.* Don't collaborate with those whom you can't trust.

2. *Partner with your opposite.* This assumes you know your strengths and are willing to collaborate with those who are strong in areas that you aren't.

3. *Know your purpose.* If you know where you are headed, you can join up with people who are on the same road.

4. *Network.* Get out and meet people. Build relationships before you even think of collaborating. Don't just build a card file of acquaintances, but get to know other people and learn what motivates them.

Obviously, this is not an exhaustive teaching on partnerships and collaborations. Instead, it is an exhortation to get out your own little world so you can learn to "play well" with others. If you want to do great things and enjoy succcccess, then there is usually no such thing as a one-man or woman act. Succcccess usually comes through strategic collaboration.

Stop going it alone and playing it safe, and learn to

partner with others so that you can enjoy the synergies of joint ventures that will allow you to reach your goals.

Commitment

The first four traits that begin with the letter C and lead to succccccess are curiosity, creativity, competence and collaboration, which we have discussed in the previous four chapters. Now let's look at the final C word that leads to succccccess, and that word is commitment.

THE WINNER IS

When I think of one standout who had to persevere while being totally committed to God's plan, the winner is Joseph in Genesis. Joseph had his visions from God indicating that he would lead his family when he was only 17 years of age. After that, all hell and parts of heaven broke loose for him and before he knew it, his brothers had sold him into slavery, then covered their deed with their family by concocting a story that Joseph had been devoured by a wild animal.

Joseph initially prospered in Potiphar's Egyptian household, and then languished in prison until he was 30 years old. At that time, Pharaoh had his two dreams, and Joseph was summoned to the palace to interpret the dreams. Joseph correctly interpreted that there would be seven bountiful years and then seven of famine. Then he suggested a plan that pleased Pharaoh of how to prepare for those lean years. Pharaoh was pleased, and Joseph went from the dungeon to the palace in a matter of minutes, although he had been a slave in Egypt for 13 years.

It the story ended there, it would be a good one—but it doesn't! Joseph served Egypt during the seven good years, storing up grain and establishing Pharaoh's throne. Then the lean years begin and Joseph's family, not knowing he was alive in Egypt, came down to buy food. They appeared before Joseph and he recognizes them, but they don't recognize him. Joseph eventually told his brothers after he identified who he was, "I will provide for you there, because five years of famine are still to come. Otherwise you and your household and all who belong to you will become destitute" (Genesis 45:11).

What's my point? Joseph was 39 when his brothers came to get food and he revealed himself to them. That means he lived in his dreams before they became reality for 22 years. Can you wait for your dream that long, preparing for the day when it will come to pass?

YOU MAY BE NEXT

If you have done all you can do, are you prepared to wait? Are you committed to whatever it takes to realize succcccess in the long run, whether that is in business, ministry, publishing or some other purpose expression? You can be the next Joseph, if you are willing to pay the price for succcccess as I have spelled out in the last five chapters. Like Joseph, you can have a long wait, but then have your life change for the better in five minutes.

As I write, I have yet to realize some of the things I believe God put in my heart. That is why I keep writing, praying, learning and growing. I am committed to do what it takes to see my dreams come true, and that may mean I see them from another vantage point after I am gone to be with Him. Whatever it takes, I won't give up. I invite you to join me in the pursuit of succcccess. Let's not stop until we run as far and fast and as long as we can, as He empowers us.

How High Can You Jump?

I have a riddle for you: In what two summer Olympic sports is the winner not awarded the gold medal until he or she has failed three times? Then I have a question: Do you know how high you can jump? Let's see if we can answer the riddle and the question, as I explain why I posed them.

THE OLYMPICS OF FAILURE

Do you know the answer to the riddle? The two sports in which you get a gold medal *after* you fail three times are the pole vault and the high jump. The last man or woman left in either competition gets to set the bar at any height, usually just over the world record, and then he or she has three attempts to try and clear that height. Once that person fails to clear three times, the competition is over and the winner is declared. This is why the world record has been broken so often in both sports because people are not afraid to fail as they discover how high they can vault or jump. I wish more people had that same attitude and played by the same rules.

You never know what you can do until you attempt to do it, but failing to attempt can simply be playing it safe because you don't want to knock down the bar, so to speak. I recently accepted some one-time opportunities to teach that kept me quite busy for an entire week. My first thought when asked to teach them was, "I am too busy to do all that." I accepted and actually taught a total of thirteen hours from Friday afternoon through Saturday evening. When I was done, I went home to bed, but I did it. What's more accurate is that God empowered me to do it.

What is God empowering you to do these days? In

other words, how high can you jump? It's not about jumping, but about service, work, or some other practical expression of your faith. Do you really know how much you can do out or the potential you have?

MOST PEOPLE WHO SAY THEY CAN, DON'T

I often hear people quote the popular passage, "I can do all things through Christ who strengthens me" (Philppians 4:13, NKJV). When you stop to think of that verse, it is only a declaration of potential. Just because you *can* do something doesn't mean you *will* do it. If I say, "I *can* be a nice person," it doesn't mean I am exercising my potential. It just means I have the potential.

When someone quotes this verse to me, I am tempted to ask, "So what are you doing?" When I do ask, the question usually makes people uneasy, for that verse is sacred to many. When I challenge its relevance, it is tantamount to heresy. Let me ask you, however, since you cannot get mad at me face-to-face: If you can do all things through Christ, what are you doing? Where and when has that supernatural strength and power enabled you to jump higher than you thought?

After my thirteen-hour teaching ordeal, I was tired, but I still had energy to write and do some household chores. I cleared the bar of teaching that was set for me and I am the better for it. What's more, the students I was able to teach are also the better for it, too.

Why not set the bar a little higher this week and see if you can clear it? Why not bless others, pray, write, study or read beyond what you thought possible and see whether or not it is possible? Why not choose to live in the truth of Philippians 4:13 and not just talk about it?

What Are You Doing Here?

In this chapter, let's look at a servant of God who was depressed and discouraged, or in the term of the day, he was "bummed out." His name was Elijah and he took refuge in a cave after a difficult time in his life to sulk and complain. His way out of his funk was to hear the voice of the Lord. If you are "bummed out," that is your way out as well.

THE VOICE OF GOD

When Elijah was sulking in his cave, this is what the Lord said to him:

> And the word of the Lord came to him: "What are you doing here, Elijah?" He replied, "I have been very zealous for the Lord God Almighty. The Israelites have rejected your covenant, broken down your altars, and put your prophets to death with the sword. I am the only one left, and now they are trying to kill me too." The Lord said, "Go out and stand on the mountain in the presence of the Lord, for the Lord is about to pass by." Then a great and powerful wind tore the mountains apart and shattered the rocks before the Lord, but the Lord was not in the wind. After the wind there was an earthquake, but the Lord was not in the earthquake. After the earthquake came a fire, but the Lord was not in the fire. And after the fire came a gentle whisper. When Elijah heard it, he pulled his cloak over his face and went out and stood at the mouth of the cave. Then a voice said to him, "What are you doing here, Elijah?" (1 Kings 19:9b-13).

When God asked Elijah what he was doing there, God wasn't looking for information. He already knew, but Elijah *didn't* know and that was the problem. Elijah was depressed because he was looking at the circumstances and not listening to the Lord.

Notice how God's voice came. It was not in the power of nature or the fire. Instead, the Lord spoke in a gentle whisper. You can't hear a gentle whisper if there is lots of other noise around you. Elijah had to block everything else out and listen to the voice that had led him up to that point in his life. It had never failed him and was not about to fail then.

WHAT ARE YOU DOING HERE?

Is the Lord asking you what he asked Elijah? Is he asking you why you are "here," wherever the here may be? If so, he knows why you are discouraged, and why you are delaying and hiding. He is not asking for His benefit but for yours! And you must do what Elijah did. You must learn to hear the voice of God, perhaps learning all over again. Perhaps Psalm 46:10-11 will help you: "Be still, and know that I am God; I will be exalted among the nations, I will be exalted in the earth." The Lord Almighty is with us; the God of Jacob is our fortress."

God is a great and effective communicator. If you aren't hearing, then the problem does not rest with Him. This week I encourage you to do what Elijah did: Get honest with yourself and God, and then be still and listen. His desire is to speak to you. Is your heart set to listen and hear? I know God will reveal Himself to you and that His presence is the key to getting out of the cave you may be in.

Fear Not!

In the previous chapter, we looked at the story in 1 Kings 19 when Elijah was depressed and discouraged in his prophetic work. He took refuge in a cave where he was hiding from the threats of Queen Jezebel. This story is similar to a situation in the life of the Apostle Paul. First, let's look a bit deeper into Elijah's story, and then move on to look at Paul.

FEAR

I did not point out in the last chapter that Elijah's problems started when he gave in to fear. He had just confronted and killed all the prophets of Baal as described in 1 Kings 18. When Jezebel threatened to kill him after that, however, he took off running:

> Now Ahab told Jezebel everything Elijah had done and how he had killed all the prophets with the sword. So Jezebel sent a messenger to Elijah to say, "May the gods deal with me, be it ever so severely, if by this time tomorrow I do not make your life like that of one of them." Elijah was afraid and ran for his life (1 Kings 19:1-3).

Imagine that! Elijah was afraid after his great victory over the false prophets, so he ran and ran. Once he stopped running, God spoke to him and sent him back to where he had come from to do the work that God had called him to do. It is interesting that the same thing happened to the Apostle Paul as we read in Acts 18:

> After this, Paul left Athens and went to Corinth. There he met a Jew named Aquila, a native of

Pontus, who had recently come from Italy with his wife Priscilla, because Claudius had ordered all the Jews to leave Rome. Paul went to see them, and because he was a tentmaker as they were, he stayed and worked with them. Every Sabbath he reasoned in the synagogue, trying to persuade Jews and Greeks.

When Silas and Timothy came from Macedonia, Paul devoted himself exclusively to preaching, testifying to the Jews that Jesus was the Christ. But when the Jews opposed Paul and became abusive, he shook out his clothes in protest and said to them, "Your blood be on your own heads! I am clear of my responsibility. From now on I will go to the Gentiles." Then Paul left the synagogue and went next door to the house of Titius Justus, a worshiper of God. Crispus, the synagogue ruler, and his entire household believed in the Lord; and many of the Corinthians who heard him believed and were baptized.

One night the Lord spoke to Paul in a vision: "Do not be afraid; keep on speaking, do not be silent. For I am with you, and no one is going to attack and harm you, because I have many people in this city." So Paul stayed for a year and a half, teaching them the word of God (Acts 18:1-11).

FEAR NOT!

Paul had just come to Corinth from Athens where he had experienced very little ministry success. The Jews became abusive and opposed Paul, so he turned his efforts to work exclusively with the Gentiles. Do you see what the Lord told Paul? He told him not to be afraid. God doesn't tell someone *not* to be afraid unless that person is already afraid. Perhaps Paul was considering moving on from Corinth, just as Elijah had moved on to avoid an encounter with Jezebel. In spite of the situation, the Lord told Paul to hold steady, for he had much work for him to do in Corinth.

Perhaps you are afraid and thinking of moving on from your current assignment? Maybe someone is opposing your work or your message. They could even be abusive and harsh. The word to you is the same as it was to Paul: Fear not! God is with you and He will not allow you to be run off from the work He has called you to do. He can't stop you from running, however, if you give in to fear and anxiety. It should give you great comfort that Elijah and Paul were fearful; it should also encourage you that they may have wavered but they never gave in to that fear—or God did not allow them to give in to it.

Are you facing opposition? Are you questioning your ability to fulfill your purpose? If you answer "yes" to either question, then I urge you to follow the example of these two great men and not surrender your life's work to the affects of fear. "Don't be afraid" is the word of the Lord to you this day, and may God strengthen you, as He did Elijah and Paul, for the great work that is yet ahead of you to accomplish.

Too Late

I ran across a quote by Martin Luther King Jr. not too long ago that impacted me deeply. Before I share that quote, however, I want to share a passage from Isaiah that people recite and even sing to me regularly (it was put to music years ago). It is their life philosophy and approach to missions, creativity and action, and it reads like this in the NAS Version:

> He gives strength to the weary,
> And to him who lacks might He increases power.
> Though youths grow weary and tired,
> And vigorous young men stumble badly,
> *Yet those who wait for the Lord*
> Will gain new strength;
> They will mount up with wings like eagles,
> They will run and not get tired,
> They will walk and not become weary
> (Isaiah 40:30-31, emphasis added).

A CLOSER LOOK

The key phrase in that passage for many is "those who wait on the Lord." The implication is that if you are going to serve the Lord, you need to wait. There is only one problem with that interpretation and application. Everything else in that passage describes action (flying, running, and walking), not waiting. And why does God need to give strength to those who "wait"? I would propose that those who wait don't need any strength—patience maybe, but not strength.

For once, the NIV is more accurate in its translation of the word "wait," for the NIV states, "but those who *hope* in the Lord will renew their strength." Replace the word wait with hope in the passage from the NAS Bible quoted above, and you will see that there is a big difference between hoping and waiting. Most already have the waiting down pat. I want to be a person who hopes as I run, fly and walk, and I invite you to join me as we run together toward our purpose and creative fruitfulness.

THE QUOTE

Now for the quote from Martin Luther King's speech "Beyond Vietnam," delivered on April 4, 1967 in New York City. I will offer no commentary on his closing comments. I trust you to draw your own conclusions and make the necessary adjustments in your life and work to apply what he said:

> We are now faced with the fact, my friends, that tomorrow is today. We are confronted with the fierce urgency of now. In this unfolding conundrum of life and history, there is such a thing as being too late. Procrastination is still the thief of time. Life often leaves us standing bare, naked, and dejected with a lost opportunity. The tide in the affairs of men does not remain at flood—it ebbs. We may cry out desperately for time to pause in her passage, but time is adamant to every plea and rushes on. Over the bleached bones and jumbled residues of numerous civilizations are written the pathetic words, "Too late." There is an invisible book of life that faithfully records our vigilance or our neglect. Omar Khayyam is right: "The moving finger writes, and having writ moves on."

Where are you waiting and doing nothing, when you should be hoping and doing something?

Criticism

Do you enjoy criticism? I don't know too many who do, but it can sometimes be an important part of your development. If you can't handle criticism and misunderstanding, then you won't go very far in your quest for purpose. Let's see if we can't learn some things about criticism that will make it a bit easier to accept the next time you encounter it.

SUCCESS BRINGS CRITICISM

When Gideon had won a great battle over the Midianites, some of his allies confronted him after his victory: "Now the Ephraimites asked Gideon, 'Why have you treated us like this? Why didn't you call us when you went to fight Midian?' And they criticized him sharply" (Judges 8:1). Gideon had fought on their behalf, but it did not prevent his friends from taking him to task.

This reminds me of another story later in the Bible when David was sharply criticized after his men's families were taken captive: "David was greatly distressed because the men were talking of stoning him; each one was bitter in spirit because of his sons and daughters" (1 Samuel 30:6a). After all David and Gideon had done, they had their critics, and you will have yours, too. With that in mind, you have three options of how to handle the inevitable criticism.

THREE STRATEGIES

First, you can become defensive, spending a lot of time and energy explaining why you did what you did. What's more, you can determine never to do much of anything again because the effort is too painful when it results in criticism. I would not recommend this first option.

Second, you can do what Gideon did:

> But he answered them, "What have I accomplished compared to you? Aren't the gleanings of Ephraim's grapes better than the full grape harvest of Abiezer? God gave Oreb and Zeeb, the Midianite leaders, into your hands. What was I able to do compared to you?" At this, their resentment against him subsided (Judges 8:2-3).

Gideon answered diplomatically and softly. He helped his critics see that their perspective was a bit skewed and that they were also an important part of what had just happened. Gideon showed restraint and wisdom, for he knew that leaders will be criticized. He deflected it and won his critics over with a gentle, non-defensive answer.

Third, you can do what David did: "But David found strength in the Lord his God" (1 Samuel 30:6b). David did not react or respond. He took some time to regain his perspective and he did that by going to the Lord. The Lord spoke to David and he returned to lead the very men who had threatened to stone him. What's more, he led them to victory.

I once thought that fear of failure was the greatest hindrance the people of God face. I now consider fear of criticism to be the number one obstacle to obedience. Since criticism is inevitable, it is vital that you develop strategies to deal with it and still remain focused and purposeful. That is what Gideon and David did and if they did it, with God's help, you can, too.

50 Years Later at 39,000 Feet

When I need inspiration or a word from God, I just need to get on a plane going somewhere, anywhere. I can't explain it, but it's a magical moment for me every time I fly, and I have logged 3.5 million miles since 1989! My love for air travel started when I was only ten years old, although it would be nine years later before I would actually get on a plane. Here's how it all began.

A FIFTY-YEAR OLD MEMORY

My family never traveled anywhere. We never took a trip longer than 40 miles from our home and we never had a family holiday or vacation together. I remember playing in my back yard as a child and looking up at the airplanes flying overhead, wondering where they were going and why we were not going there. Then one day my life changed forever.

During some time off from work, my father told me that he was taking me somewhere but it was a surprise. We got in our car and drove 32 miles to visit, not fly out of but just *visit*, the Greater Pittsburgh Airport. When we drove into the old airport (they have since built a new one), it had huge, elaborate fountains that changed colors at night. The airport itself had a variety of shops, great-tasting popcorn, a movie theater, a game arcade and an observation deck. This was probably in 1960.

Most of the planes landing and taking off were of the propeller variety, but I remember standing on that observation deck and watching them start up, take off and land. I was fascinated. We got there in the early evening and found out a jet plane was coming in from Chicago at 9 p.m., which was the

71

time of the summer sunset. Dad said we could wait for the jet to come in and we did.

I will never, *ever* forget using the deck's binoculars to watch that TWA jet approach and land while there was still some daylight. I was absolutely spellbound and speechless. When we left after spending three hours there, I said to myself as a ten-year old boy, "I will be on one of those planes one day." I have fulfilled my vow over and over again.

WHAT ARE YOUR MEMORIES?

That story is part of who I am. That visit helped shaped my life. Dad had no idea that our simple trip to the airport would make such an impact on my life. I cannot ever forget that 50-year-old memory, nor do I want to do so.

What experiences like I described have shaped your life? Are you being true to the impact of those events? If not, how can you re-connect with those things that helped make you the person you are today? Was it a concert, a family trip, a museum, summer job, visit to a hospital or movie? What was it about that event or experience that made it so special?

If you reflect on that event, you may discover some clues to your purpose that will help discover the riddle of your life purpose. Even if that memory was decades ago, it may not be too late to do something about what you had only once dreamed of doing. I would write more, but it's time for me to get on a plane, and you now know what a special event that is for me—and why.

You Don't Have Time

There are two types of people in the world of productivity. There are those who say they don't have enough time and they don't. Then there are those who say they don't have enough time and they don't. Confused? You should be, for I have defined two separate groups with the identical phrase. What could I possibly mean by this? Ah, to find out, you will have to read on.

GROUP ONE

The first group doesn't get things done that they would like to do because they are waiting for conditions to be just right before they move forward. They are waiting to have the mortgage paid off, the children to be grown and gone, their retirement years to arrive, or to have a ton of money saved in the bank. Then there are others who are waiting for unrealistic chunks of time to become available before they even start on their goal or dream.

Someone once said to me, "I wish I could go off for about eight weeks and do nothing but write! Then I could get something done." I replied, "You don't know what you are asking. If you ever have eight free or uninterrupted weeks to do something, that means you have lost your job, broken your leg or are recovering from a heart attack!" The people in this group remind me of what the wisdom writer had to say: "Whoever watches the wind will not plant; whoever looks at the clouds will not reap" (Ecclesiastes 11:4).

Some of those in group one are perfectionists; others are fearful that they can't produce or do what they want, so they use the excuse that they don't have time to prevent them from ever starting or seriously planning.

GROUP TWO

Then there is group two who says they don't have time and they are correct—they really don't! This group, including yours truly, usually tries to shoehorn four hours work into two hours. We can't say "no," so we tend to overcommit, believing that all things are possible for those who work hard and are called according to His purpose (a slight variation on Romans 8:28). Our to-do list is as long as our arm and even then we feel like we are underachieving.

For group one, the solution is to be realistic. No one usually has huge blocks of uncommitted time, so they must learn to use what they have. This group must also deal with their unrealistic perfectionism, which says that only the perfect is good enough in every situation. This group would do well to heed the verses immediately following the verse mentioned above:

> As you do not know the path of the wind, or how the body is formed in a mother's womb, so you cannot understand the work of God, the Maker of all things. Sow your seed in the morning, and at evening let not your hands be idle, for you do not know which will succeed, whether this or that, or whether both will do equally well (Ecclesiastes 11:5-6).

For group two, the solution is also a dose of realism. If they are doing to do some of the things we want to do, they must stop doing some of the things they are currently doing. For example, there is only one way I could go back to school when I was 57 years old, and that was to stop traveling as much as I was. There are only 24 hours in a day and no matter how organized or committed I was, there are limitations. Where are those limits? I don't know; that's what you and I have to find out. For group one, the answer to their challenge is a to-do list; the answer for group two is a *stop* to-do list.

I know which group I am in. Into which group do you

fall? It would be good to find out and then take steps this week that will enable you to do some of the things that are important to you and that are in your heart to do. Discover why you don't have enough time and then find the proper mindset that will enable you to produce. The answer is either to be busier so you can use the time you have or to be less busy so you can use the time you have. Have fun figuring out which one applies to you.

You Are the Problem

You may be the greatest obstacle you face in your quest for purpose. It's not the economy, your education, how much money you have, or your age. The problem isn't any of those things. The problem is you. More specifically, it's the way you think.

What's more, you are probably trying to change yourself while holding on to old thought patterns, expecting different results while you think the same thoughts. You are seeking a personal transformation, focusing your energy on changing your habits, knowledge, spiritual disciplines or place of employment. If you are the problem, then wherever you go and whatever you do, you take the problem with you, along with your old thought habits. When that happens, even if you pray or read the Bible more, you won't see any difference in your life.

You need to change your mind if you are going to change yourself. Your old thinking won't take you to new places. It's that simple, but the process can be difficult.

SEND THEM HOME

In Matthew 14, Jesus had taught a large crowd of people in a remote place:

> As evening approached, the disciples came to him and said, "This is a remote place, and it's already getting late. Send the crowds away, so they can go to the villages and buy themselves some food." Jesus replied, "They do not need to go away. You give them something to eat" (Matthew 14:15-16).

What was the problem here? Was it the lateness of

the hour? Was it the lack of food that the disciples had? Was it that the crowd, in their zeal to follow Jesus, had not given enough thought about what they would eat?

The problem was this: The disciples' thinking too small and, consequently, they only saw one option available to them at that moment. They suggested that Jesus dismiss the meeting and send the people home. Jesus had another idea and that was to take what the disciples had, bless it and then feed the people with that. We know that this is what He did and the crowd of 5,000 plus women and children were fed with twelve baskets of leftovers. When you think too small, you do what the disciples did: you dismiss your opportunities because you don't think you have what it takes to seize the moment.

WE STILL CAN'T DO IT

Do you think the disciples learned their lesson? They did not! In the next chapter, we read how they complained to Jesus that there was no way they could feed a smaller crowd with the little they had (see Matthew 15:29-39). Jesus did the same thing He did in Matthew 14 and fed the crowd with the little food in their possession. The disciples were still stuck in their old patterns of thinking, and that limited their creativity and ability to solve the problem that was before them.

Are you any different than those disciples? The challenge isn't what you have and don't have. It's how you think about what you have and who you are. If you don't think you can, then you won't. What's more, you won't even try. If you think you can or if you think *God* can through and with you, then God will plant new ideas and thoughts in your mind, just like He did with the disciples when He said, "*You* give them something to eat."

Paul was clear about the importance of your thinking. If you are going to be transformed, you must do so by renewing your mind (see Romans 12:1-2). That won't happen, however, unless you take steps to make it happen. You must learn to be ruthless with your old thoughts that have gotten you nowhere and replace them with thoughts that can take you somewhere, thoughts full of faith and possibilities, not thoughts full of defeat and pessimism.

You must become aware of what you are thinking. Pay attention to your thoughts and listen to what you say. Be more conscious of how you are limiting yourself, or how you are limiting what God can do with the loaves and fishes in your possession. As you do, you will see the need to develop new thinking habits that will in turn transform your life into the victorious, glorious experience that intended for it to be.

Your Board of Directors

There are two statements in two different epistles that seem to contradict one another. The first statement is found in John's first epistle: "As for you, the anointing you received from him remains in you, and you do not need anyone to teach you. But as his anointing teaches you about all things and as that anointing is real, not counterfeit—just as it has taught you, remain in him" (1 John 2:27).

The second statement is found in Paul's letter to the Ephesians, in which Paul declared that teachers are numbered among the "big five" of ministry positions: "It was he who gave some to be apostles, some to be prophets, some to be evangelists, and some to be pastors and teachers" (Ephesians 4:11).

John wrote that we don't need a teacher, but Paul stated that teachers are critical to my development as a believer. Which one is correct? How can we resolve this contradiction? To find out, of course you must read on.

JOHN WAS RIGHT

John wrote his letter to some who had teachers telling them that Jesus was not the Christ. John labeled those teachers liars, telling the reader that they knew better. The "anointing" inside them taught them and bore witness that Jesus was indeed who He said He was. The presence of the Spirit in those believers also told them that those false teachers were in error. There were some things, according to John, that believers knew because the Spirit of truth resided in their hearts. They had no need for anyone to confirm or teach them.

One of those things believers "know," in my experience, is the truth about their purpose. No one can assign you a purpose. It is in you and, when you hear or see it, it rings true. I would say it is part of the "anointing" that John refers to, for it is something that is personal and directly assigned by the Lord Himself. That anointing not only allows you to know your purpose, it also helps you fulfill your purpose. At the same time, your purpose increases your need for the Church and the "big five," which includes pastors and teachers. You can't stand alone once you find what only you can find and know – your purpose.

PAUL WAS RIGHT, TOO

As usual, there is no contradiction in the Bible on this point. There are some things you know, like your purpose, but there are other things you need to learn, like doctrine, right behavior and values. Your purpose sets you apart, but your need for coaches, mentors and teachers makes you part of a team, and that team is often found in the church. This doesn't mean that your purpose isn't relevant in the world of business, medicine or education. It does mean that you won't be as effective as you could be if you don't embrace those in the church who are assigned to instruct and guide you in the ways of God.

I hope you aren't waiting around for someone to tell you what your purpose is. That is something only you can find out and only you can recognize when it comes. At the same time, if you know your purpose, I hope you are a part of a team that can help equip and train you to be effective and relevant. Purpose is personal but how you express it is not, and that's where some miss it. Often no one can help you find your purpose but many can help you fulfill it.

I have written in the past about your need for a personal board of directors, people who are living or dead who can train and teach you. Who is on your board of directors? Who inspires you to better performance? Who challenges you to grow and develop? Who helps clarify your values and then helps insure that you live them? This would be a good time to first clarify your purpose and then to recognize and formalize your team of teachers and mentors who give you life and direction. Make a list of who they are, or make a list of who you would like them to be. Don't be confused, however, about their role. Only *you* can find your purpose but only *they* can help make it all that God wants it to be.

I Am What I Am, and You Are, Too

My weeks are almost always busy and full of purposeful activity, and recently I was reminded of something that happened to me when I was in a busy season 30 years ago. The lessons I learned then have served me well and I thought I would share them with you in this chapter. What are those lessons? I'm glad you asked, but to find out you will have to read on.

SOMETHING HAS TO GO!

Twenty years ago I was busy and involved in way too many projects, or so I thought. I decided to spend some time seeking the Lord to determine what I could and should eliminate from my calendar and life. I was certain that something had to go.

I prayed, listened, and kept a journal, yet nothing happened. I got neither relief nor insight. Then one night I had a dream. I don't remember the dream; I only remember that a voice spoke to me in the dream and gave me a verse from the Bible. I clearly heard someone in the dream mention 1 Corinthians 15:10. I was not familiar with that verse and had no idea what it said until I looked it up: "But by the grace of God I am what I am, and His grace toward me did not prove vain; but I labored even more than all of them, yet not I, but the grace of God with me."

I continued to pray and journal, and God made the meaning clear to me. He wasn't going to send any less for me to do. He was actually going to send *more*, but was also going to teach me how to handle more. He did, I have and the lessons I learned from that verse continue to bear fruit 30 years later.

THE LESSONS, PLEASE

Here's what I learned:

1. *By the grace of God I am what I am.* People inquire regularly how I am able to do what I do. My standard is answer is that I stopped doing what I can't do so that I can do what I do best. Who made me a good administrator? God by His grace. Who did not create me to be a Sunday-morning pastor? God by His grace. Who made me with a love for sports and a good sense of humor? God by His grace. I decided back after the dream that if anyone had a problem with who I am, that's their problem. i cannot use that as an excuse for bad behavior or rudeness, but I can use it as a foundation upon which to live my life.

2. *His grace toward me did not prove vain.* This particular phrase showed me something remarkable. I can be the recipient of God's grace, yet receive it in vain! You can talk about God's purpose, swim in God's purpose, write about it, and meditate on it. Yet your purpose is meant to make you productive in the will of God, nothing more, nothing less. I don't know how many days I have left to live, so I want to maximize them all. I am grateful for God's grace and I want His grace to yield a return that will be pleasing to Him.

3. *I labored more than all of them.* God wants me to be a model of productivity and hard work. I am not to engage in any hard work, but labor that is related to my purpose and sphere of influence. From 2001 to 2008, I lived in Africa six months a year. During one of those years, I spent 22 nights on a plane flying somewhere. I did all that because God wants me to work hard and produce! He has taught me both how to manage and also have faith for time, and I know I can squeeze as much out of 24 hours as anyone. I do this not because I *have* to but because I *choose* to. It is joy for me.

4. *Not I, but the grace of God with me.* My hard work and productivity cannot be a source of pride, nor can I impose my workload or expectations on someone else. It is what God

has for me to do. I cooperate and partner with God. Yet if He wasn't with me, helping me every step of the way, I would not be able to do anything, as the psalmist reminds me: "Unless the Lord builds the house, its builders labor in vain. Unless the Lord watches over the city, the watchmen stand guard in vain. In vain you rise early and stay up late, toiling for food to eat— for he grants sleep to those he loves" (Psalm 127:1-2, NAS).

There you have my lessons learned from 1 Corinthians 15:10. Why don't you meditate on that verse and see how you can apply it to your current life situation? Do you feel like you're too busy? Are you as productive as you would like to be? Do you sense God's grace helping you on a daily basis? Have you learned to have faith for time? All these are important questions to consider until you find answers. I did, and the fruit of my insight from that verse has served me well and will continue to do so until my days are over.

A Bad Leader Can Teach You to be a Good Leader

Have you ever been in a bad situation, one from which you could not escape or see any reason for being there? If you have been or are currently, then you are in good company, for King David was in a difficult relationship with King Saul. Yet God had put David in that scenario, for it was part of God's development plan for David as one of the greatest leaders the world has ever known. Let me explain.

A BAD LEADER

We can all agree on the fact that King Saul wasn't a good leader. He started strong, but he ended miserably. Saul and David began their relationship as close as father and son, but Saul quickly became David's nemesis. Even though David faithfully served Saul, Saul was increasingly envious of David and ultimately tried to kill David on three separate occasions. When those attempts failed, Saul spent years using the armies that should have been fighting the Philistines to hunt down David.

David suffered greatly during that time. Although David knew he was to be the next king, he had to endure persecution at the hand of the current king. Some of his followers urged David to take matters into his own hands and remove Saul, and others tried to act on his behalf. David resisted each temptation to dethrone Saul and punished those who tried, choosing rather to wait for God to put him on the throne rather than put himself there.

Why would God put David in such a position? Why

did David suffer so long at the hands of a man that God had rejected as king? What was God doing during that time?

It's clear what God was doing. God was teaching David how to lead from a firsthand example of a bad leader. David learned more about leadership from Saul than from anyone else. What did he learn? He learned how not to lead! Can this be the answer to your current dilemma, which finds you far away from the fulfillment of a purpose that you understand and are ready to embrace?

TALK IS CHEAP

There are some who say, "If I was in charge, this would happen or that would not happen." That kind of talk sounds good. Even the leaders in Jesus' day said the same thing: "And you say, 'If we had lived in the days of our forefathers, we would not have taken part with them in shedding the blood of the prophets'" (Matthew 23:30).

The problem is that this talk is cheap. If you don't decide what kind of purposeful leader you will be *before* you have money or power, you are doomed to replicate the same miserable leadership style that you had to endure to become a leader yourself. You don't believe me? Read what Jesus said in response to those potential leaders: "Therefore I am sending you prophets and wise men and teachers. Some of them you will kill and crucify; others you will flog in your synagogues and pursue them from town to town." (Matthew 23:34).

God will eventually give you a chance to lead, just like He did David. David learned his lessons under Saul well and mapped out what kind of leader he was going to be while Saul was still pursuing him. What's even more important, David actually *became* that kind of leader. Jesus' contemporaries duplicated the same mistakes of the past because they didn't learn good leadership skills from their bad leaders. When they refused to learn, they were doomed to repeat history.

Why are you where you are right now? Why is your situation so tough? Part of the reason may be so that you will learn how *not* to lead when you finally get the chance. If people are being stingy with you, learn to be generous now. If no one expresses thanks to you now, remember how it feels and express gratitude when you are in charge.

If that's what God is teaching you, then you can embrace your current situation more enthusiastically because it simply part of your training. When you learn the lesson, God will move you on. Don't be guilty of saying today that things will be different when you are in charge, only to continue to model your leadership after the tyrant who oppressed you. Make a difference when you eventually have the chance to do so. If and when you do that, the hard lessons of those days will be well worth the price you paid to become the leader that God wants you to be.

Purpose Is Not Enough

I regularly meet with people to help them find their life purpose, and I am always thrilled when I see the concept of purpose break through in someone's thinking. I am working on some Internet options that will allow my purpose experience to impact even more people all over the world. There seems to be no ebb in people's desire to find and fulfill their purpose.

In the previous chapter, we looked at the prophet Daniel. Daniel was a success both as a prophet as an administrator in Babylon not only because of his gift and anointing, but also because he was faithful: "They could find no corruption in him [Daniel], because he was trustworthy and neither corrupt nor negligent" (Daniel 6:4). Daniel had skill but he also had integrity, and they go hand in hand if you are going to fulfill your God-given purpose.

A BIG MISTAKE

For all my emphasis and teaching on purpose, I find that many people make a crucial mistake in life, work and ministry. They believe the power of purpose or a creative idea is enough to ensure success. If you are serving God, however, you cannot overlook faithfulness, sowing, service and your heart attitude as important means through which you will succeed in your purpose.

There is a passage in Luke 16:10-12 that is critical to your life and purpose success:

> Whoever can be trusted with very little can also be trusted with much, and whoever is dishonest with very little will also be dishonest with much. So if

you have not been trustworthy in handling worldly wealth, who will trust you with true riches? And if you have not been trustworthy with someone else's property, who will give you property of your own?

Here are some questions to consider from that passage:

1. *Are you faithful in little things?* This can include things like punctuality, follow-through on promises and all the other "little things" that can easily be overlooked in the busy-ness of life. As "small" as they are, Jesus said they are important, because if you are dishonest with those little things, you will act the same with the more important things.

2. *Are you faithful with money?* This would include giving something to the Lord's work when you have the chance, paying your bills on time, paying back money you borrow from others, and being free from greed and theft.

3. *Can you handle someone else's property as your own?* This includes being faithful with a business or church opportunity that belongs to another. For example, if you borrow something, you return it in better shape than you received it. If you quote someone, you give them credit.

A PARTNERSHIP

Yes, knowing your life purpose is vital to life success, but so are integrity and stewardship. God is watching you, and He does not bless and promote solely on the basis of potential or a good idea. God looks at the heart and He promotes anyone whose heart belongs to Him, which means those who will work and act like Jesus. You need purpose but it needs to partner with faithfulness if God is going to use you.

If we haven't already, maybe one day we will meet to talk about purpose. Don't be fooled, however, into thinking that purpose will guarantee your success. It's an important step in the process, but you cannot ignore Jesus' words in Luke 16 and expect to get very far in business or ministry. God is watching, and you had better make sure that your character matches the size of your purpose vision. Where God is concerned, purpose just isn't enough.

Daniel Was What He Didn't Eat

In this chapter, I want to talk a bit about the life of Daniel. Both Daniel and Joseph are two "super heroes" in the Old Testament. They are almost too good to be true. They were faithful in the midst of temptation and loyal in the spite of persecution and trials. Both men are worthy of our study and emulation, but for now, we will focus only on Daniel.

MOST LIKELY TO SUCCEED

In some American high schools, graduating seniors designate one of their classmates whom they deem most likely to succeed in the future. Daniel didn't go to an American high school, but if he had, he would have been given that honor. Consider the kind of young people that King Nebuchadnezzar was looking for to serve in his kingdom: "Young men without any physical defect, handsome, showing aptitude for every kind of learning, well informed, quick to understand, and qualified to serve in the king's palace" (Daniel 1:4).

Since Daniel was chosen, we know that he qualified based on the listed criteria—smart and good-looking. Daniel had a bright future in his homeland of Judah, but God had other plans. While still a teenager, Daniel was whisked off to Babylon, selected for royal duty, and given a three-year crash course in Babylonian culture.

What was involved in this crash course? Daniel was sent to language school. He was assigned a new name. Beltheshezzar. which contained the name of one of the main Babylonian gods, Bel. He was then placed under the care of the chief of the eunuchs. Now I ask you: Why would Daniel be under this man unless they had made Daniel a eunuch himself? Here was a bright young man, with his whole future ahead of him, but suddenly he's living in a foreign land, called by the name of a foreign god, learning a strange new culture, and facing a future that didn't include a wife and family!

In spite of all that, Daniel distinguished himself throughout his Babylonian career. He was a man of skill and efficiency and also penned a book in the Bible that carries his name. What enabled this man to be so successful?

DANIEL WAS WHAT HE DIDN'T EAT

Daniel was a man of purpose, but he was also a man of values. When he first arrived in Babylon to become a royal official, he was also assigned royal rations that he was to eat. Daniel refused: "But Daniel resolved not to defile himself with the royal food and wine, and he asked the chief official for permission not to defile himself this way" (Daniel 1:8). If I am a teenager, having gone through all that Daniel had been through, the last thing I would have been concerned with was eating the local food. Daniel remembered the dietary laws of a Jew, however, and he determined to maintain a kosher diet even in Babylon. As a young man, Daniel knew what was important to him and he was determined to follow those values no matter what.

The most impressive thing about Daniel had such well-defined values at an early age. The second most impressive thing is that he was committed to follow them, even in a foreign land after his life had been turned upside down. Have you defined your values? If so, do you think you could follow them if you went through what Daniel went through? I'm not sure that I could.

Your assignment this week is to do some work to define your values. If they worked for Daniel, they will work for you. I have an article outlining how to do this in the Appendix entitled "How to Develop Your Governing Values." Spend 60 minutes giving thought and expression to what is important to you. Once you do, don't be content for those values only to exist on paper, but find a way to live them out in good times and in bad. Your values are essential to your quest for purpose, which we will discuss more in the chapter to follow.

Peter's Purpose Profile

God is often more comfortable with our humanity than we are. What I mean by this is that we let our failures and what we *can't* do keep us from doing what we *can* do. This wasn't the case with Peter. He made many mistakes, spoke out of turn and actually denied that he knew the Lord. Yet Peter was the one who stood up when the Holy Spirit fell at Pentecost and led thousands of people to Jesus. He was also one of the first Jews to go to the Gentiles and begin the revival that made it possible for you and me to serve the Lord. Yes, Peter was imperfect but he was a purpose champion for God because he did not allow his frailty to stop him.

You can be a purpose champion too, but you must not allow your imperfections and mistakes to prevent you from fulfilling your purpose. I have encountered many people who are working to improve their weaknesses, not attempting anything for God until they or their circumstances improve. If you are doing that, you have adopted a flawed strategy. In all probability, God is less concerned with your failures than you are. Are you more righteous than God? Can you have higher standards than God has? You're only human and not perfect or superhuman. Stop trying to be either. If Peter left a purpose legacy, so can you. If God is willing to work in and through you, then let Him.

AN IDENTITY RUT

When Jesus met Peter, his name wasn't Peter but rather Simon (see Mark 3:16). Jesus changed his name and today we don't refer to Peter as Saint Simon. Why do you think Jesus changed Peter's name? Perhaps Jesus wanted Peter to see himself differently. Jesus became not only Peter's Lord, but also his ministry coach. Coach Jesus decided that Peter needed a new perspective of who he was. From that point on, therefore, Peter was known as Peter, which translated means the rock.

Peter received a new identity and Jesus expected him to walk in it. Every time someone said Peter's name, it was a reminder of who Peter was, not who he had been. Do you dwell on the past? Are you bogged down in an old image that others assigned to you and that you accepted? For many years, I was known as an administrator because that was what my job was. When I began to position myself as a speaker and consultant, some didn't recognize me and others opposed me, not willing or able to receive this new image and identity. I then had a choice: Was I going to revert to that old identify or forge ahead in my new one? I chose to forge ahead, yet some still refuse to accept me for who I am, clinging instead to who they knew me to be previously.

Are you stuck in an identity rut? Do some refer to you as Simon, while Jesus knows you as Peter? If that's the case, you have a choice to make. Whose report will you believe? Those who want to keep you as Simon, or Coach Jesus who wants to free you to be the person He knows you can be? That's an important but sometimes difficult choice to make. I pray you will have the courage to accept your Peter identity and shed your Simon label.

STUDY YOUR RESUME FOR CLUES

When Jesus met Simon Peter, he was working in his family business as a fisherman:

> When Simon Peter saw this, he fell at Jesus' knees and said, "Go away from me, Lord; I am a sinful man!" For he and all his companions were astonished at the catch of fish they had taken, and so were James and John, the sons of Zebedee, Simon's partners. Then Jesus said to Simon, 'Don't be

afraid; from now on you will catch men." So they pulled their boats up on shore, left everything and followed him (Luke 5:8-11).

Once again we see that Simon Peter was hung up in his past, telling Jesus that he was sinful—as if Jesus didn't already know that already! When you spend time reminding God of your sins, do you really think He is interested? Do you think He has forgotten? That isn't the point, however, I want to make. Simon Peter was a fisherman. His job held a clue to his purpose. Jesus knew that Peter's purpose was similar to his employment, for Peter would become fishers of men, harvesting them for God's kingdom. On the one hand, Jesus was trying to set Peter free from his past, and on the other hand, Jesus was helping Peter see how part of his past was closely related to his future.

Does your employment history hold clues to your purpose? Don't be too quick to say "no." Do you have a resume? Study it and ask yourself some questions: What did I enjoy about that job? What did I hate? What was absent from the jobs I hated? Is there any common theme or activity among all your jobs? What feedback did you get during your job evaluations? Study the answers and see if there is any pattern that you can see.

LET'S REVIEW.

What did we see in Peter's life in this chapter that will help you with your own quest for purpose?

1. If God is willing to work in and through you, let Him. Don't allow your mistakes or weaknesses derail your PurposeQuest.

2. Don't accept any other identify except the one that Jesus has for you.

3. Study your job history to see if it holds any clues to help you in your PurposeQuest.

Purpose Questions

When I first began teaching about purpose, I made every effort to derive my material from the Bible. If I could not find purpose there, then I was not going to continue my quest to know more. That led me to develop what I called "purpose profiles" of individuals whose stories were included in the Bible's narratives. In this chapter, we begin a five-part series that examines the purposeful life of Nehemiah. Before you continue, you may want to read the book of Nehemiah.

In short, Nehemiah served the Persian king Artaxerxes, who ruled from 464-424 BC. In about 445 BC, Artaxerxes commissioned his servant Nehemiah to return and rebuild Jerusalem, the city of Nehemiah's fathers. This profile will study how Nehemiah got assigned to duty in Jerusalem and what he did once he was there. Of course, we will see that Nehemiah was a man of purpose or he could not have done the great work that he did.

The book of Nehemiah begins with Nehemiah asking some men who had just come from Jerusalem some questions: "In the month of Kislev in the twentieth year, while I was in the citadel of Susa, Hanani, one of my brothers, came from Judah with some other men, and I questioned them about the Jewish remnant that survived the exile, and also about Jerusalem (Nehemiah 1:1-2).

The point I want to make is that *you probably don't know your purpose because you don't ask enough questions.* I heard a motivational speaker say one time that quality questions lead to a quality life. What he meant was that you must seek the truth concerning who you are, and part of the seeking process is asking the right questions.

Nehemiah was interested in Jerusalem and its residents, even though he had never been there. One day a group of travelers from Jerusalem stirred his interest and Nehemiah asked a lot of questions. Their answers provoked him to prayer and thoughtful action. The rest is history.

When I first discovered my purpose, it was because I asked God, "If you didn't create me to start this business that failed, what *did* You create me to do?" That was a quality question. The Lord responded, "I made you to create order out of chaos!" That was a quality answer, the pursuit of which has led me to a quality life, one that enables me to do what I love all over the world. What questions are you currently asking? If quality questions lead to a quality life, do no questions lead to a nothing life? Do you continue to ask until you get an answer or some clarity on the matter?

Here are three good questions to ask as you seek your purpose. Work on these and there will be more in the chapters to come.

1. What would you do with your life if you had all the money you needed to live on?

2. What compliments have you regularly heard that may hold clues to your purpose?

3. What gives you the greatest joy?

There is no way to force the Lord to give you answers, and sometimes He does not respond because you are not ready to hear what He has to say. That's why it's so important to keep on asking, for sometimes God must prepare the ground of your heart to receive the purpose seeds. What's more, when you keep asking, you exercise faith that God will reward you for your diligence. In the next chapter, we will continue our Nehemiah profile, but the lesson for you now is to ask and keep on asking good questions, trusting that you will obtain good answers.

Purpose Tears

In the previous chapter, we continued our purpose profile series with a lesson from the purposeful life of Nehemiah. The first point we made in the previous chapter was:

1. *You don't know your purpose because you don't ask enough questions—and keep on asking until you get an answer.*

Now, let's move on and focus on the second purpose lesson from Nehemiah's life.

WHAT MAKES YOU CRY?

When Nehemiah heard the answers to his questions to the visitors about the conditions in Jerusalem, he was deeply moved: "When I heard these things, I sat down and wept. For some days I mourned and fasted and prayed before the God of heaven" (Nehemiah 1:4-5).

Sometimes I substitute the word passion for purpose. Passion is a driving force that activates your creativity and will to do something. Tears of joy and sorrow often accompany that passion as you respond and make yourself vulnerable and available to a need that exists in the world. The first time I spoke about purpose, people in the room wept. I have seen hundreds more cry over the years. Tears and purpose seem to go together hand in hand.

In 1998, I was watching a television documentary about the suffering women in Afghanistan and I began to cry. I remember asking, "Lord, why am I crying? I don't know anyone there but if you need someone to go to Afghanistan, I'm willing." Out of the blue in 2003, I received an invitation to go to Afghanistan from people I didn't even know. I went and it changed my life and the course of my ministry.

The second purpose point we can learn from Nehemiah is this: *2) Tears go hand-in-hand with purpose.* What makes you cry? I'm not referring to tears of sorrow when a loved one passes or when you receive bad news. Can you sit and listen to a certain type of music and cry? Do you cry during a sad movie? Cry with joy when someone is blessed? If you do, then ask the Lord questions like, "Why am I crying? What was touched in me that moved me to tears? What does it mean, Lord?" The answers may surprise you and hold clues to clarify your purpose. It certainly did for Nehemiah.

Purpose is not just a head thing, it's a heart thing. You need to involve your entire being as you search for purpose. That means you must pay attention to your feelings—it's called self-awareness—and seek reasons for what you are thinking *and* feeling. Purpose triggers joy and sorrow in your life; that's why those two emotions are so important in discovering your purpose. Don't ignore those two factors, and don't consider them signs of weakness. Instead, use them as launching points that will thrust you into the world of purpose where you will do what you are passionate about doing.

Purpose Clarity

I teach in a graduate-level organizational leadership program and we focus on Nehemiah as a model leader. I am always surprised at the fresh, new insight the students regularly have into Nehemiah's story. I have found it to contain a treasure trove of material about purpose, and that will be our focus for this chapter.

WELL, I SORT OF, YOU KNOW, KIND OF LIKE...

Nehemiah prayed and fasted to clarify his passion and his life direction from it. After he sought the Lord, his big breakthrough came. One day he was serving the king who noticed that Nehemiah was sad. Let's read the rest in Nehemiah's own words.

> The king said to me, "What is it you want?" Then I prayed to the God of heaven, and I answered the king, "If it pleases the king and if your servant has found favor in his sight, let him send me to the city in Judah where my fathers are buried so that I can rebuild it." Then the king, with the queen sitting beside him, asked me, "How long will your journey take, and when will you get back?" It pleased the king to send me; so I set a time.

> I also said to him, "If it pleases the king, may I have letters to the governors of Trans-Euphrates, so that they will provide me safe-conduct until I arrive in Judah? And may I have a letter to Asaph, keeper of the king's forest, so he will give me timber

to make beams for the gates of the citadel by the temple and for the city wall and for the residence I will occupy?" And because the gracious hand of my God was upon me, the king granted my requests. So I went to the governors of Trans-Euphrates and gave them the king's letters. The king had also sent army officers and cavalry with me (Nehemiah 2:4-9).

The third point is that you must be able to state your purpose and goals with clarity and conviction. When the king asked Nehemiah what he wanted, Nehemiah had a ready answer. The king clearly understood, and could then either say "yes" or "no."

People often ask me questions to help clarify their purpose. At times, I ask them what they *think* their purpose is. It's then that I see just how hard it is for some people to talk about themselves. They will often say, "Well, I think my purpose is, sort of, like to help people. Yeah, that's it. And I probably, you know, encourage other people, but of course it's not me, it's the Lord."

Does that sound like clarity? You can't state your purpose and preface it with phrases like "I think," "probably," or "maybe." You either know your purpose or you don't. If you can't overcome the natural hesitancy that many have talking about themselves, you will always struggle to come up with a clear statement.

LET'S REVIEW

In this series so far, we have learned three purpose lessons from Nehemiah's profile. They are:

1. *Most people don't know their purpose because they don't ask enough questions*

2. *Tears often go hand in hand with purpose*

3. *You must be able to state your purpose and goals with clarity and conviction.*

In the next chapter, we will continue our Nehemiah profile. Before you go there, I want you to get your notebook, journal or a sheet of paper, and write down all the questions you can think of concerning your purpose. Write them all down, even if one question is, "What should I be asking?" I ask you to do this in order to focus your search by posing good questions. By doing so, you will have a better chance of obtaining good answers. Then, get comfortable not only talking about what you can't do, but also what you can do. Your objective is to be able to clearly answer anyone who asks, "What is your passion and purpose?"

Your Purpose Enemies

In this chapter, let's continue the purpose profile of Nehemiah to see what we can learn to help each of us in our quest for purpose. Nehemiah faced a lot of opposition as soon as he began to rebuild Jerusalem, and that is the fourth point we can learn from Nehemiah's PurposeQuest: *You will always face opposition when you seek to fulfill your purpose—some of it from without, some from within.*

> When Sanballat heard that we were rebuilding the wall, he became angry and was greatly incensed. He ridiculed the Jews, and in the presence of his associates and the army of Samaria, he said, "What are those feeble Jews doing? Will they restore their wall? Will they offer sacrifices? Will they finish in a day? Can they bring the stones back to life from those heaps of rubble-burned as they are?" Tobiah the Ammonite, who was at his side, said, "What they are building-if even a fox climbed up on it, he would break down their wall of stones!" (Nehemiah 4:1-3).

That's how it is with people of purpose: your enemies don't show up until you get serious about doing God's will. Nehemiah wasn't the only one to face purposeful opposition. Joseph faced the enmity of his brothers when he shared his dreams with them. David incurred the wrath of Saul and the disinterest of his family after David was anointed king. Daniel was a faithful public servant in Babylon, but then his opponents conspired against him that ultimately had him sent to the lions' den.

Jesus didn[1]t have an enemy in the world until He preached and healed on the Sabbath. After He did, there was a group of men dedicated to see Him die. Your enemies are actually a sign that you are doing something *right*, not that you are doing something wrong. The Apostle Paul was a devoted Jew who then preached that Jesus was the Messiah. After that, old friends and even family became his enemies, some devoted to his assassination.

FEAR OF CRITICISM

I formerly considered the fear of failure as the most significant obstacle we face in fulfilling our purpose. I have changed my mind and now consider the fear of criticism as the greatest challenge. Sometimes our greatest source of criticism is from those who are closest to us. They become a purpose opponent because they think they know our purpose better than we do. They are threatened when we step out to do something, or they want to protect us from disappointment and hurt. Whatever their reason, those closest to us can be our most significant purpose obstacle because we fear their criticism.

As you seek to fulfill your purpose, where is your greatest source of external opposition? Is it from family, friends or associates? Identifying what you do that attracts the greatest opposition may give you a significant clue concerning your purpose. In the next chapter, we will talk about what attracts the most internal opposition from your own heart and mind, but for now, reflect on what you do that seems to rile people up the most. See if that insight can help you clarify your purpose and in the next chapter we will continue our look at Nehemiah.

Your Purpose Legacy

Let's finish up in this chapter with our purpose lessons from Nehemiah's narrative. In the previous chapter, we looked at the tendency for enemies to appear when you start to pursue and fulfill purpose. External opposition is serious, but it may not be the most serious obstacle where your purpose is concerned. It is the opposition from *within* that is often the most crippling. Fear, doubt and anxiety all serve to disable and render you useless where purpose is concerned.

That is our fifth point in Nehemiah's PurposeQuest: *Your purpose is bigger than anything you can accomplish by yourself.* You can read Nehemiah's own account of the internal opposition the people faced: "They were all trying to frighten us, thinking, 'Their hands will get too weak for the work, and it will not be completed.' [But I prayed,] 'Now strengthen my hands'" (Nehemiah 6:9).

Nehemiah's enemies threatened him, and the people who were with him were fearful. Nehemiah recognized what was going on and prayed for God to strengthen him. If you behold the need and then assess your ability, you will probably say to God, "I cant do this! Im not smart or gifted enough. Help me, Lord!" When you clarify your purpose, you realize that you can't fulfill your purpose in your own strength.

When I went to Afghanistan in 2003, I said "no" to the invitation three times. I didn't have the time, money or energy to go, or so I thought. I should have recognized, however, that all those things only proved that it was God's will for me to go; I faced the internal opposition of fear, doubt and inadequacy. All those simply caused me to trust God all the more, so I went. What is it that causes you the greatest fear and doubt? Could that be telling you about your purpose?

PLAN YOUR OWN FUNERAL

Stephen Covey wrote the classic book, *The 7 Habits of Highly Effective People.* His second habit is "begin with the end in mind." To do that, Covey recommended that you write your own funeral eulogy today. His reasoning was that you must be doing today what it is that you want to be remembered for tomorrow. And that is the sixth point we can learn from Nehemiah's life is: *Your purpose is the legacy you want to leave behind.*

- "*Remember* me with favor, O my God, for all I have done for these people" (Nehemiah 5:19).

- "*Remember* me for this also, O my God, and show mercy to me according to your great love" (Nehemiah 13:22).

- "*Remember* me with favor, O my God" (Nehemiah 13:31, emphasis added).

I want to be remembered as a writer; therefore, I must write books. I want to be a man who was organized, which allowed him always to have time for people. That has caused me to study organizational skills and develop them. Do you get the point? Nehemiah prayed for God to remember Him. He desired his legacy to be more than a statue; he wanted to be remembered as one who did great things for God. God heard his prayer, for here we are, 2,500 years later, talking about Nehemiah's legacy. God did remember him!

What do you want to be remembered for? What positive comments do you want people to make at your funeral? The answers to those questions will provide additional insight into your purpose, for they help you identify what is truly important in your life.

LET'S WRAP IT UP

As we finish our Nehemiah profile, let's look at the points we learned by studying his life:

1. Many people don't know their purpose because they don't ask enough questions.

2. Tears often go hand in hand with purpose.

3. You must be able to state your purpose and goals with clarity and conviction.

4. You will always face opposition when you seek to fulfill your purpose.

5. Your purpose is bigger than anything you can accomplish by yourself.

6. Your purpose is the legacy you want to leave behind.

Those six points give you a lot to think about as you continue your PurposeQuest. Take those points and write down the insights you receive as you meditate on them. Don't take mental notes; the ink fades too quickly. Keep a purpose notebook or journal and record your thoughts, prayers and insights. As you do, you will develop your own purpose profile that will encourage and help guide others. If I can be of assistance, don't hesitate to write.

Your Shadow

There is a concept in the study of psychology called your shadow. It is an aspect of your personality of which you are unaware or choose to ignore, but that doesn't mean it isn't active. People may encounter your shadow side every time they come in contact with you, traits like your sarcasm, competitiveness, need to control, fear, or need for attention. You can see why you tend to ignore those things, for they are in no way positive at all. Until you can bring those shadows into the light, they continue to operate and can damage your relationships, work and ministry.

Did you realize, however, that you also have a more shadow? It's the positive effects you leave whenever people have an encounter with you. While the psychological shadow is usually harmful, your spiritual shadow can be positive and leave a lasting impact for good. You are undoubtedly familiar with the Apostle Peter's negative shadow, his weakness that led him to deny the Lord after insisting he would *never* do that. You may not be as familiar with his positive shadow that is described in Acts 5:15: You can read about the Apostle Peter's positive shadow: "People brought the sick into the streets and laid them on beds and mats so that at least Peter's shadow might fall on some of them as he passed by."

This verse seems strange to some, but I take it to heart and pray that the same dynamic will be present in my life: "Lord, help me recognize my negative shadow, so my positive one—all the encounters I underestimate or aren't even conscious of with others, can impact them for your purpose and glory!" Will you join in that prayer and then work to maximize every encounter you have with others for Him?

There is one other example of a positive shadow that is worthy of your attention. Look at this unusual story found later in Acts: "God did extraordinary miracles through Paul, so that even handkerchiefs and aprons that had touched him were taken to the sick, and their illnesses were cured and the evil spirits left them" (Acts 19:11-12). People went into Paul's workshop, took his work apron, allowed people to touch it and they were healed. That leads me to another prayer: "Lord, I want my work to touch people whether I am present or not. Use my life—my writing, speaking, teaching, and every other activity—in a way that brings healing to peoples' lives, whether physical, emotional or spiritual!"

My goal is to be a God-carrier wherever I go and in whatever I do. I want my shadow and my work—the extension of my purpose—to go with me, before me and remain after me so God can use them for His purpose. If that means I must make myself personally available for people to touch my shadow or my apron, so be it. My life is His and I will not worship at the altar of privacy if God wants me to go public. Join me in praying those two prayers, and then develop your shadow and your work to such an extent that God can use them both to bring healing to hurting people who have been wounded by the negative shadow —their own and that of others.

Who Are You?

I want to ask you a simple question and then help you come up with an answer because you will probably struggle with the answer. The question is, "Who are you?" When John the Baptist broke onto the Judean scene, he created quite a stir among all the people, especially the leadership. They immediately dispatched a delegation to ask that very question about his mission and purpose:

> Now this was John's testimony when the Jewish leaders in Jerusalem sent priests and Levites to ask him who he was. He did not fail to confess, but confessed freely, "I am not the Messiah." They asked him, "Then *who are you?* Are you Elijah?" He said, "I am not." "Are you the Prophet?" He answered, "No." Finally they said, *"Who are you?* Give us an answer to take back to those who sent us. *What do you say about yourself?"* John replied in the words of Isaiah the prophet, "I am the voice of one calling in the wilderness, 'Make straight the way for the Lord'" (John 1:19-23, emphasis added).

If John had not known his purpose, he could have easily succumbed to the definitions that were being presented. They tried to make him the Messiah, Elijah and the Prophet. John steadfastly refused to be seen or defined through the eyes of others, but had a ready answer for those who challenged his work: He had come to prepare the way for the Lord. That statement represents his purpose, and it was biblical and practical. What's more, he had plenty of evidence to back it up, for people were streaming to visit and submit to his baptizing ministry.

Do you have the same kind of clarity that John had? What do you do when people press you for answers as to who you are, what you do best and what are you here to do? If you respond with vague generalities like, "I am here to do God's will" or "I exist to glorify God," then you will leave people no choice but to define you on their own. If you are afraid of purpose specificity, then you may be content to be known by others' labels. I am not.

In the coming days, spend some time rehearsing your answers to the questions: *Who are you? What do you say about yourself?* Take a long look at whether or not you have allowed others to answer those questions for you, or if you have answered those questions for yourself. Are your answers clear? Do they keep you focused when others are pressuring you to be someone else? Are they so clear that others can describe who you are on your behalf?

John the Baptist impacted Israel, not because he tried to be everything to everyone, or to fulfill others' expectations. He did so because he was a man of purpose. You will do well to follow in his footsteps and to have a ready answer for the world who wants to know who you are. God wants you to know as well, so armed with that knowledge, seek to be clear and consistent when confronted with the question, "Who are you?"

A Deep Sleep

I once heard a pastor preach an excellent word on Jonah, and I had an insight into the concept of rest as he was speaking—even though rest was not the focus of his message. This chapter will focus on another aspect of Jonah's story—that he was asleep when the storm hit his escape ship:

> Then the Lord sent a great wind on the sea, and such a violent storm arose that the ship threatened to break up. All the sailors were afraid and each cried out to his own god. And they threw the cargo into the sea to lighten the ship. But Jonah had gone below deck, where he lay down and fell into a *deep sleep* (Jonah 1:4-5, emphasis added).

Jonah was trying to use sleep as a means to hide from the Lord and the consequences of fleeing his purpose! Perhaps Jonah thought if he slept, he would not be conscious to any remorse or guilt over his rebellion. Jonah was in such a deep slumber that the captain of the ship had to awaken him to ask incredulously, "How can you sleep?" Perhaps Jesus, the Captain of your ship, is asking you the same question, *how can you sleep when:*

- you don't know how many more days you have to fulfill your purpose?
- the God of the universe has given you an assignment only you can do?
- there are so many depending on you to fulfill your purpose?
- the world is dying and you have life?

- you have known for some time that God has given you something to do?

You can sleep or retreat into rest if you are scared or if you are in rebellion, like Jonah was. You can try to play the rest "trump card," seeing if God will exempt you from service, but I doubt it will work. Contrast the idea of rest with Paul's testimony of what it took for him to fulfill his purpose:

> Rather, as servants of God we commend ourselves in every way: in great endurance; in troubles, hardships and distresses; in beatings, imprisonments and riots; in hard work, *sleepless nights* and hunger; in purity, understanding, patience and kindness; in the Holy Spirit and in sincere love (2 Corinthians 6:4-5, emphasis added).

Dear friend, is there a storm brewing around you, but you are in a deep sleep? Is the Captain asking you how you can sleep at a time like this? Are you fatigued not from action, but from inaction, missing the joy and energy of God to propel you through whatever you are assigned to do? The good news is that God isn't angry and He is willing to get you where you need to be, just like Jonah in the belly of the fish, once you throw yourself into the storm and trust God. Read Jonah's story again in Jonah 1 and 2, and then awaken from your place of rest to a place of action. I promise you God will give you all the rest you need, but first you have to earn it. You cannot use that rest as an escape.

That Means You

In John 14:12, Jesus made this astounding promise: "I tell you the truth, anyone who has faith in me will do what I have been doing. He will do even greater things than these, because I am going to the Father." In your opinion, what was the greatest thing that Jesus did? When I aske that, most people respond that it was when He raised the dead. If that's true, then what could be a greater work than raising a dead person? Raising more dead people? Clearing out a cemetery or hospital?

Many people don't think much about this verse in John 14 because they don't believe that they can surpass what Jesus did, regardless of what they consider to be His greatest works. If you think like that, however, then you miss a dynamic that could greatly help you be more productive.

Jesus did fabulous things but there were some things He *didn't* do. Jesus never opened an orphanage. He never wrote a book. As far as we know, He never founded a hospital or organized a group to go on a mission of mercy to a foreign land. He never started a business and never gave a large sum of money to a worthy cause. Why didn't He do those things? He didn't do them because He left those things for you and me to do.

YOUR GREATER WORKS

Therefore, if you believe in Jesus, and I assume you do, why aren't you doing greater things than He did? Perhaps you have underestimated how important and powerful it would be to actually achieve the things that are in your heart today. You may also think that only a supernatural miracle would

qualify as a greater work. Since you don't perform supernatural miracles, you assumed that John 14:12 was for someone
else and you were exempt or disqualified from this tremendous
promise.

I have faith in Jesus and I want to do greater works.
How about you? If you answer "yes," then what will you do?
Where can you apply your faith so that the results are mi-
raculous? Maybe you will care for AIDS orphans or perhaps
you will open a chain of businesses. You can create some educational innovation that will revolutionize the way children
learn. You may invent some technique that will make life easier
for others, enriching yourself in the process. Then you'll start
foundations like Mr. Kellogg, Mr. Ford or Mr. Rockefeller that
will fund humanitarian projects long after you're gone.

I hope you get my point. You may ask, "Who am I to
think about doing those things?" If you believe in Jesus, the
answer is, "Who are you *not* to think like that?" The question
you have to settle is whether or not John 14:12 only applies to
a select few or to every believer, including you. If it's for you,
then you have some work to do. The good news is that you're
not alone if your work is coupled with faith. With faith, you
are guaranteed that your results will be great, greater than you
could ever imagine because God is with you.

THE SOMEONE IS YOU

What have you said *someone* ought to do? Could that
someone be you? Write down in your journal what I call your
elegant dream. You don't have to know how you will do it right
now; you simply have to know what it is. Let it flow out of you
in its entirety. Once you write it out, study it. Let it become
a part of your thinking every day, and envision it as already a
reality.

If there is something you can do to make that elegant
dream a reality, what would it be? Do you need to go back to
school? Do you need to have money to do achieve your elegant
dream? Are you sure that's your greatest need? You may meet
someone soon who can help you develop a plan or give you the

money for this dream that could eventually qualify as a John 14:12 greater work. You have to be able, however, to articulate that dream, before you can expect anyone to understand it and respond, and that may start with you accepting John 14:12 as possible not just for others but also for you. What are you waiting for? Get moving, and have a great life proving the truth of that mind-boggling promise in John 14.

Tell Your Story

As I was preparing to teach a class, Psalm 105:2 caught my attention. It's a verse you are probably familiar with, but what struck me is that the verse is an exhortation for you (and me) to publish and broadcast! You may not see it like that, but let me give you a little more background. First, here is the verse: "Let the redeemed of the Lord tell their story—those he redeemed from the hand of the foe" (Psalm 107:2).

Do you have a story? You probably do, for God has done great things for you just as He has for me. That is what's known as our testimony and we are to tell it. One place to do so in church, but in today's modern church services, there is seldom time allowed to testify. That means you (and I) must find other ways to tell God's story as it has unfolded in our lives. That is where publishing, social media and the like come in. I don't often use social media for personal things, but I use it regularly to "publish" what God is showing me and what I am learning. I do my best every day to tell my story. What about you?

After I noticed Psalm 107:2, I did a little more research and discovered two interesting things in Scripture that go along with that verse from Psalms. One is in Deuteronomy 31:19: "Now write down this song and teach it to the Israelites and have them sing it, so that it may be a witness for me against them." God instructed Moses to write a song and teach it to Israel. The song's theme was to remind Israel of God's faithfulness in a day when they would go astray, but I had never noticed that God commanded Moses to be creative and write music. Do you have any music in you that needs to be written? That is another way of telling your story.

The second verse I found was in Joshua 18:4: "Appoint three men from each tribe. I will send them out to make a survey of the land and to write a description of it, according to the inheritance of each. Then they will return to me." God had commanded the spies who were sent out to submit a report in writing of what they saw in the Promised Land. Their story was not what God had done, but what God was going to do when they entered the Land He was giving them. Like the spies, part of your story is your faith vision of what is yet to come.

These verses provide three reasons to publish, write, and create: 1) to tell your story of what God has done for you; 2) to remind you and others of God's faithfulness; and 3) to report what you see pertaining to God's purpose and plan for you that is yet to be. What you have experienced in your life is not unique. There are others who are experiencing or will experience the same things. Your story can help them make it through their tough times, or encourage them to overcome timidity so they can do God's will. If you have something that can help another, then God commands you to share it. That includes your story. Don't judge what you have as irrelevant; allow God to use it for His purpose and glory.

The Importance of Your Presence

False humility involves denying your ability to do something well so you don't appear to someone else as braggadocious or proud. While this appears spiritual to some, it actually dishonors the Lord who created you to do certain things well. It also causes you to minimize your strengths and purpose in your own mind and consequently in the minds of others.

The false humility usually leads to spiritual passivity, a lackadaisical attitude that says, "There should be no hurry or urgency in the things God has given me to do. I can wait." Worse yet is the attitude that your presence and purpose really doesn't contribute much, so whether or not you act is of little consequence—God will get His will done through someone else.

That, my friend, is a dangerous and erroneous attitude that deprives God's kingdom of your presence and the results that only you can produce. Your presence is essential to God's purpose, and I am thinking of two biblical examples to prove my point.

POINT ONE

One is found in 2 Kings 3:14 where Jehoshaphat had forged an alliance with wicked Ahab and they went to see counsel from Elisha the prophet. This is what Elisha said when they came into his presence: "As surely as the Lord Almighty lives, whom I serve, if I did not have respect for the presence of Jehoshaphat king of Judah, I would not pay any attention to you." Because of Jehoshaphat's presence, Elisha went on to prophesy what would happen when those kings went into battle. The point is: the word of the Lord would not have been released had Jehoshaphat not been personally present. There are also some things that will not occur unless you are present.

POINT TWO

The second is the almost humorous story of the sons of Sceva who were trying to cast out demons in Jesus' name. When those sons took on more than they could handle, this is what the demons said to them: "Jesus I know, and Paul I know about, but who are you?" (Acts 19:15b). The demonic world was aware of Paul and, when someone tried to do what only Paul and others like him had the authority to do, the demons turned on the sons of Sceva and beat them badly.

The point from that story is there are some things that only you can do and your presence in certain situations is absolutely necessary for God's work and will to be done. As you can see, point two is the same as point one.

CONCLUSION

The conclusion is that you must learn to take the power and importance of the purpose you carry seriously and not dismiss it lightly or treat it with a nonchalant attitude. There are people and situations waiting for you to show up to do what only you can do. When you think that your presence isn't important, the opportunity is lost. Yes, God will raise up someone else to do His will in the long-run, but for today, you have work to do that only you can do and your presence is essential for that work to get done.

You may think, "I must wait on the Lord" and that's certainly important to do. Once you have found your purpose and see your divine assignment, however, the waiting is over. It's time to act and act you must, for you carry purpose power and authority that cannot be replicated or replaced. You need to change your thinking where false humility and passivity are concerned and act this minute to do the work that only you can do. Your presence is important. Now go find out where you are supposed to be and make the difference there that only you can make.

Proper Perspective

I have written in the past about the practice of false humility and the harm it does to your purpose and productivity. When you deny the fact that you can do something well (false humility), you are talking yourself out of its importance and of your urgent need to do (or be) it more. While it seems spiritual to act with a lack of urgency, a passive attitude, and self-deprecation, it often hinders, and can even thwart, God's ability to use you. I ran across a well-known quote from the Scottish poet Robert Burns, which states:

> *Oh that the gods*
> *The gift would gi'e us*
> *To see ourselves*
> *As others see us*

We see the need to see ourselves as others see us when we are acting like jerks, which does happen from time to time. I contend, however, that the need to see ourselves as others see us is greater in regards to our strengths and purpose, and not only in our sin and weakness.

MIGHTY WARRIOR

When the Lord appeared to Gideon in Judges 6, this is how He greeted him: "The Lord is with you, mighty warrior" (Judges 6:12). It's interesting that Gideon was *not* acting like a mighty warrior at the time; he was cowering in fear as he threshed wheat in a spot hidden from his enemies. Gideon went on to engage in false humility, telling the Lord: "Pardon me, my lord,' Gideon replied, "but how can I save Israel? My clan is the weakest in Manasseh, and I am the least in my family'" (Judges 6:15).

You have probably reacted just as Gideon did, and I know I have, too.

God had something for Gideon to do that only he could do. God saw Gideon's potential when Gideon did not, either because he was unable or he refused. At this point, you may say, "Well, that was what God saw and He knows everything." When God sees it (the it being your giftedness, power or potential), however, others do as well. Note later what someone said as they interpreted a dream another person had described as it pertained to Gideon:

> Gideon arrived just as a man was telling a friend his dream. "I had a dream," he was saying. "A round loaf of barley bread came tumbling into the Midianite camp. It struck the tent with such force that the tent overturned and collapsed." His friend responded, "This can be nothing other than the sword of Gideon son of Joash, the Israelite. God has given the Midianites and the whole camp into his hands" (Judges 7:13-14).

It wasn't just God who saw Midian's potential; others saw it as well.

OTHERS SEE IT

There are times when you need to see yourself as others do when you are misbehaving. It is more important, however, that you see yourself as others see you in the power of your purpose. Paul wrote about this matter when he said: "For by the grace given me I say to every one of you: Do not think of yourself more highly than you ought, but rather think of yourself with sober judgment, in accordance with the faith God has distributed to each of you" (Romans 12:3). He warned not to think more highly of yourself than is appropriate but he did not say you should accurately assess your strengths and gifts.

Where are you dismissing your power because you have been taught that it's the spiritual thing to do? Where has it caused you to be passive instead of aggressive in the revealed will of God for your life? Maybe you need to harken to prophetic words you have received, or seek out a trusted mentor, or listen to the encouragement that others are giving you. Whatever you need to do, I urge you to do it, stop acting like false humility is spiritual and get about the work of accurately assessing the importance and power that God has bestowed upon you for His purpose and glory.

About
John W. Stanko

John founded a personal and leadership development
company, called *PurposeQuest*, in 2001 and today travels
the world to speak, consult and inspire leaders and people
everywhere. From 2001-2008, he spent six months a year
in Africa and still enjoys visiting and working on that
continent. Most recently, John founded Urban Press, a
publishing service designed to tell stories of the city, from
the city and to the city. John is the author of 75 books.

Keep In Touch With John W. Stanko

www.purposequest.com
www.johnstanko.us
www.stankobiblestudy.com
www.stankomondaymemo.com

or via email at johnstanko@gmail.com

John also does extensive relief and community development work in Kenya. You can see some of his projects at www.purposequest.com/donate

PurposeQuest International
PO Box 8882
Pittsburgh, PA 15221-0882

Additional Titles In The *Unlocking* Series By John W. Stanko

Unlocking the Power of Your Creativity
Unlocking the Power of Your Productivity
Unlocking the Power of Your Purpose
Unlocking the Power of Your Thinking
Unlocking the Power of Your Faith

More Books by John Stanko

A Daily Dose of Proverbs

A Daily Taste of Proverbs

Changing the Way We Do Church

I Wrote This Book on Purpose

Life Is A Gold Mine: Can You Dig It?

Strictly Business

The Faith Files, Volume 1

The Faith Files, Volume 2

The Faith Files, Volume 3

The Leadership Walk

The Price of Leadership

What Would Jesus Ask You Today?

Your Life Matters

Live the Word Commentary: Matthew

Live the Word Commentary: Mark

Live the Word Commentary: Luke

Live the Word Commentary: John

Live the Word Commentary: Acts

Live the Word Commentary: Romans

Live the Word Commentary: 1 & 2 Corinthians

Live the Word Commentary: Galatians, Ephesians,
Philippians, Colossians, Philemon

Live the Word Commentary: 1 & 2 Thessalonians,
1 & 2 Timothy, and Titus

Live the Word Commentary: Hebrews

Live the Word Commentary: Revelation

Ediciones en Español

Cambiando la Manera de Hacer Iglesia

La Vida Es Una Mina De Oro: Te Atreves A Cavarla?

No Leas Estes Libro: (A Menos Que Quieras Convertirte E Un
Mejor Líder)

Fuero lo Viejo, Adentro lo Nuevo

Gemas de Propósito

Ven a Adorarlo: Preparándonos para Emmanuel

www.ingramcontent.com/pod-product-compliance
Lightning Source LLC
Chambersburg PA
CBHW060209070426
42447CB00035B/2879